Teacher Guide
Passwords
Social Studies Vocabulary
United States History: The Constitution to 1920

S0-BLT-448

Developer: Maureen Devine Sotoohi

Writer: DeVona Dors

Cover Design: Susan Hawk

Photo Credits: Front cover: clockwise from top left James Steidl/Shutterstock.com; The Granger Collection, New York; Library of Congress, Prints & Photographs Division, LC-DIG-ppmsca-13484; ©Bettman/CORBIS

Reviewers: Curriculum Associates, Inc. would like to acknowledge the contribution of the educators who reviewed *Passwords* at various stages of its development. Their insightful comments have made our program a better one for teachers and students.

Gracie Alvear
Bilingual/ESL/Immigrant Student Service
Elementary Supervisor
Edinburg CISD
Edinburg, Texas

Jackie Baldwin
Secondary Reading Senior Coordinator
Instructional Services Division
Polk County Schools
Bartow, Florida

Lorraine Cruz
Principal
Ames Middle School
Chicago, Illinois

Leonila Izaguirre
Bilingual-ESL Director
Pharr-San Juan-Alamo ISD
Pharr, Texas

Judy Lewis
Director, State and Federal Programs
Folsom Cordova Unified School District
Folsom, California

Dominique Mongeau
Categorical Program Adviser
Carson Street Elementary School
Los Angeles Unified School District
Carson, California

⏶CURRICULUM ASSOCIATES®, INC.

Table of Contents

ISBN 978-0-7609-4709-8
©2008—Curriculum Associates, Inc.
North Billerica, MA 01862
Permission is granted for reproduction of the reproducible pages
in limited quantity for classroom use.
All Rights Reserved. Printed in USA.

15 14 13 12 11 10 9 8 7 6 5 4 3 2 1

Overview

Passwords: Social Studies Vocabulary is designed to build the vocabulary essential to understanding the key concepts students are studying in social studies. The topic areas and vocabulary words used in ***Passwords: Social Studies Vocabulary*** have been chosen based on the social studies standards developed by individual states. The topics and vocabulary words also align with the basal social studies textbooks of major publishers.

Passwords: Social Studies Vocabulary is recommended for all students who need practice with the vocabulary that will help them succeed in social studies. These students may include English language learners as well as other striving learners. See pages 9–11 of this teacher guide for vocabulary teaching strategies that will help teachers meet the needs of all their students.

The lessons in ***Passwords: Social Studies Vocabulary*** are grouped by topic area, and each lesson may be taught independently. Teachers may choose to go through the book lesson by lesson. Alternatively, they may select individual lessons that correspond to the topic being taught in class. By providing an overview of grade-appropriate topics, ***Passwords: Social Studies Vocabulary*** may also be used to help students prepare and review for standardized tests in social studies.

The ***Passwords: Social Studies Vocabulary*** student book reading selections are available on an audio CD. The CD is a useful tool to use with English language learners or other students who would benefit from listening to the reading selection multiple times. Auditory learners will find listening to the selections on the CD especially helpful.

Use this product *right away, the right way!* e-Training for Teachers
CAtraining.com

Student Books

Passwords: Social Studies Vocabulary student books have been written and designed to provide students with a text that is "considerate," or reader friendly. Three hallmarks of considerate text are clear text structure, coherent writing, and audience appropriateness. *Passwords: Social Studies Vocabulary* incorporates these characteristics of considerate text into every lesson.

Clear Text Structure

The reading selections in *Passwords: Social Studies Vocabulary* feature text structures that exhibit clear organizational patterns. In descriptive text, information is given in a logical order of importance. For sequential text, events are presented in the order in which they occur. In cause-and-effect text, the relation between the actions or events is clearly stated.

Coherent Writing

The social studies concepts and ideas presented in *Passwords: Social Studies Vocabulary* are clearly stated. An introductory paragraph states the topic of the lesson. All the information in the reading selection connects to the topic. No extraneous material confuses readers. Headings and subheads highlight the cohesion of each text segment. Transitional words and phrases signal the relation between actions or concepts.

Audience Appropriateness

Although the readability of *Passwords: Social Studies Vocabulary* reading selections is below grade level, the concepts and material in the selections are grade appropriate. Prereading activities activate students' prior knowledge. Activities that follow the reading selection help teachers evaluate student understanding.

Look for these signs of considerate text in the *Passwords: Social Studies Vocabulary* student books.

- Short line length for increased readability
- Simple sentence structure
- Paragraphs with clear topic sentences and relevant supporting details
- Introductory subheads
- Target vocabulary words boldfaced in text
- Definitions of target vocabulary words near the first use of the word
- Simple font
- Clean page layout
- Appropriate, not overwhelming, visuals
- Illustrations support content

The student book for **United States History: The Constitution to 1920** has 15 lessons. Each lesson introduces and practices ten key vocabulary words related to a single social studies topic.

Features of the Lesson

Each lesson of the student book contains these features:

- Target Vocabulary
- Lesson Opener
- Reading Selection
- Graphics
- Activities A–D
- Word Root
- Write!

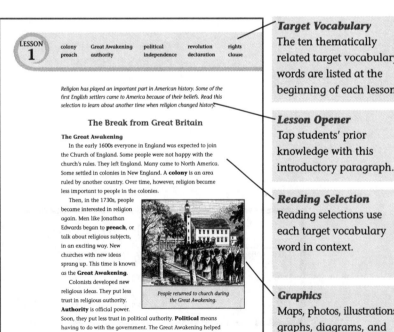

Target Vocabulary
The ten thematically related target vocabulary words are listed at the beginning of each lesson.

Lesson Opener
Tap students' prior knowledge with this introductory paragraph.

Reading Selection
Reading selections use each target vocabulary word in context.

Graphics
Maps, photos, illustrations, graphs, diagrams, and charts expand and enhance meaning.

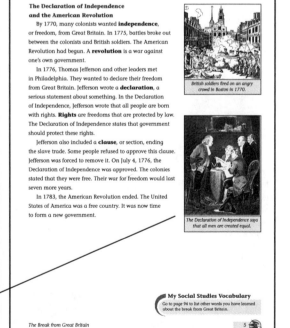

Progressively difficult activities follow
each reading selection.

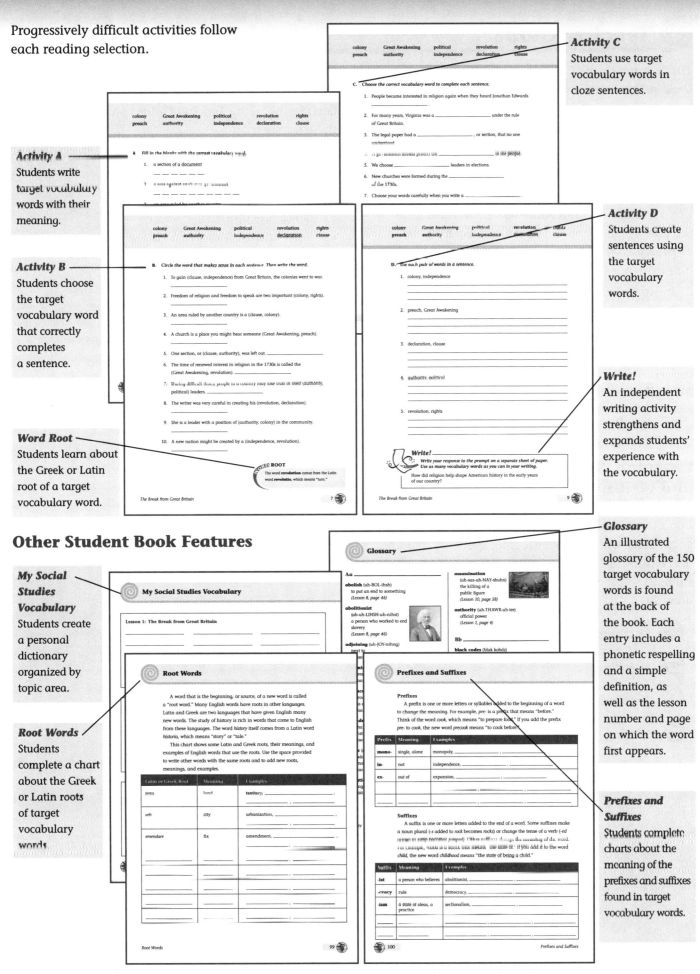

| colony | Great Awakening | political | revolution | rights |
| preach | authority | independence | declaration | clause |

C. Choose the correct vocabulary word to complete each sentence.

1. People became interested in religion again when they heard Jonathan Edwards _____.

2. For many years, Virginia was a _____ under the rule of Great Britain.

3. The legal paper had a _____, or section, that no one understood.

4. A government should protect the _____ of the people.

5. We choose _____ leaders in elections.

6. New churches were formed during the _____ of the 1730s.

7. Choose your words carefully when you write a _____.

Activity C
Students use target vocabulary words in cloze sentences.

| colony | Great Awakening | political | revolution | rights |
| preach | authority | independence | declaration | clause |

A Fill in the blanks with the correct vocabulary word.

1. a section of a document
   _ _ _ _ _ _

2. a war against an already-in-power government

3. an area ruled by another country

Activity A
Students write target vocabulary words with their meaning.

Activity B
Students choose the target vocabulary word that correctly completes a sentence.

| colony | Great Awakening | political | revolution | rights |
| preach | authority | independence | declaration | clause |

B. Circle the word that makes sense in each sentence. Then write the word.

1. To gain (clause, independence) from Great Britain, the colonies went to war. _____

2. Freedom of religion and freedom to speak are two important (colony, rights). _____

3. An area ruled by another country is a (clause, colony). _____

4. A church is a place you might hear someone (Great Awakening, preach). _____

5. One section, or (clause, authority), was left out. _____

6. The time of renewed interest in religion in the 1730s is called the (Great Awakening, revolution). _____

7. During difficult times, people in a country may lose trust in their (authority, political) leaders. _____

8. The writer was very careful in creating his (revolution, declaration). _____

9. She is a leader with a position of (authority, colony) in the community. _____

10. A new nation might be created by a (independence, revolution). _____

Word Root
Students learn about the Greek or Latin root of a target vocabulary word.

WORD ROOT
The word **revolution** comes from the Latin word **revolutio**, which means "turn."

| colony | Great Awakening | political | revolution | rights |
| preach | authority | independence | declaration | clause |

D. Use each pair of words in a sentence.

1. colony, independence

2. preach, Great Awakening

3. declaration, clause

4. authority, political

5. revolution, rights

Activity D
Students create sentences using the target vocabulary words.

Write!
Write your response to the prompt on a separate sheet of paper. Use as many vocabulary words as you can in your writing.
How did religion help shape American history in the early years of our country?

Write!
An independent writing activity strengthens and expands students' experience with the vocabulary.

The Break from Great Britain 7

The Break from Great Britain 9

Other Student Book Features

My Social Studies Vocabulary
Students create a personal dictionary organized by topic area.

My Social Studies Vocabulary

Lesson 1: The Break from Great Britain

Glossary

Aa

abolish (uh-BOL-ihsh)
to put an end to something
(Lesson 8, page 46)

abolitionist
(ab-uh-LIHSH-uh-nihst)
a person who worked to end slavery
(Lesson 8, page 46)

adjoining (uh-JOY-nihng)
next to

assassination
(uh-sas-uh-NAY-shuhn)
the killing of a public figure
(Lesson 10, page 58)

authority (uh-THAWR-uh-tee)
official power
(Lesson 1, page 4)

Bb

black codes (blak kohdz)

Glossary
An illustrated glossary of the 150 target vocabulary words is found at the back of the book. Each entry includes a phonetic respelling and a simple definition, as well as the lesson number and page on which the word first appears.

Root Words
Students complete a chart about the Greek or Latin roots of target vocabulary words.

Root Words

A word that is the beginning, or source, of a new word is called a "root word." Many English words have roots in other languages. Latin and Greek are two languages that have given English many new words. The study of history is rich in words that come to English from these languages. The word *history* itself comes from a Latin word *historia*, which means "story" or "tale."

This chart shows some Latin and Greek roots, their meanings, and examples of English words that use the roots. Use the space provided to write other words with the same roots and to add new roots, meanings, and examples.

Latin or Greek Root	Meaning	Examples
terra	land	territory, _____
urb	city	urbanization, _____
emendare	fix	amendment, _____

Prefixes and Suffixes

Prefixes

A prefix is one or more letters or syllables added to the beginning of a word to change the meaning. For example, *pre-* is a prefix that means "before." Think of the word *cook*, which means "to prepare food." If you add the prefix *pre-* to *cook*, the new word *precook* means "to cook before."

Prefix	Meaning	Examples
mono-	single, alone	monopoly, _____
in-	not	independence, _____
ex-	out of	expansion, _____
		_____

Suffixes

A suffix is one or more letters added to the end of a word. Some suffixes make a noun plural (*-s* added to *rock* becomes *rocks*) or change the tense of a verb (*-ed* added to *jump* becomes *jumped*). Other suffixes change the meaning of the word. For example, *-hood* is a suffix that means "the state of." If you add it to the word *child*, the new word *childhood* means "the state of being a child."

Suffix	Meaning	Examples
-ist	a person who believes	abolitionist, _____
-cracy	rule	democracy, _____
-ism	a state of ideas, a practice	sectionalism, _____

Prefixes and Suffixes
Students complete charts about the meaning of the prefixes and suffixes found in target vocabulary words.

Root Words 99

100 *Prefixes and Suffixes*

Teacher Guide

The Teacher Guide for *Passwords: Social Studies Vocabulary* contains resources that may be used to introduce, support, and extend students' vocabulary studies. The Teacher Guide includes guided instruction for each student book lesson.

Multistep Lesson Plan

Passwords: Social Studies Vocabulary is built upon the premise that students benefit most from the direct instruction of vocabulary. Each lesson as presented in the Teacher Guide follows a multistep lesson plan.

1. Introduction of the target vocabulary
2. Activation of students' prior knowledge
3. Definition of the meaning of unknown words
4. Student creation of visual representations using graphic organizers
5. Additional practice with the target vocabulary
6. Activities that help students retain the word and its meaning

Listening, Speaking, Reading, and Writing

Passwords: Social Studies Vocabulary provides opportunities for students to practice the target vocabulary words while listening, speaking, reading, and writing. These icons indicate opportunities for students to use the vocabulary words in different domains.

 Listening

 Speaking

 Reading

 Writing

Features of the Guided Teaching Lessons

Each lesson of the Teacher Guide contains these features:

- Target Vocabulary with definitions
- Cognates
- Vocabulary Strategy
- Lesson Summary
- Before Reading
- Word and Definition Cards
- Reproduced student book pages
- During Reading
- After Reading
- Annotated student book activity pages
- Extensions
- Ideas for introducing the Write! activity
- Sample answer for Write!
- Word Root extension

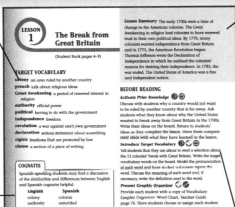

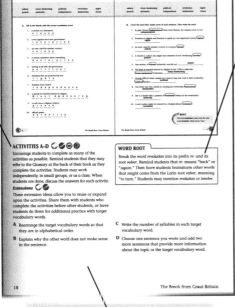

Other Teacher Guide Features

- **Vocabulary Teaching Strategies**
  Information and tips about how to employ vocabulary teaching strategies that have proven effective with struggling learners and English language learners begin on page 9.

- **Research Summary**
  A summary of the research that forms the basis of *Passwords: Social Studies Vocabulary* is on pages 12–15.

- **Reproducibles**
  Pages 76–128 of the Teacher Guide contain reproducibles for you to share with students.

  ### Graphic Organizers
  You may either photocopy the graphic organizers for students to use or use the sample graphic organizer as a model for students to create their own. The Before Reading section of each guided lesson suggests a particular vocabulary graphic organizer to use with the lesson. The Write! section of each guided lesson suggests a writing graphic organizer to use with the Write! activity.

  - **Vocabulary Graphic Organizers**

    Word Chart   This graphic organizer asks students to write the word, define it, provide examples, use the word in a sentence, and draw a picture.

    Vocabulary Map   Students write a target vocabulary word in the center box. In the outer boxes, they write a definition, the word's parts of speech, its root, and prefixes and suffixes. Students also draw a picture illustrating the word and write a sentence using the word.

    Four Square   In this graphic organizer, students write a target vocabulary word in the center rectangle. As they read, they complete the graphic organizer by drawing a picture, listing examples, writing a definition, and using the word in a sentence.

    Vocabulary Circle   Students write the target vocabulary word in the center circle and then add additional information in the outer sections.

  - **Writing Graphic Organizers**

    Topic Web   A topic web may be used with a variety of types of writing. Generally, students write the topic of their writing in the upper circle of the web and important points about the topic in the lower circles.

    Sequence Chart   A sequence chart provides students with a visual representation of the steps in a process. In this organizer, they record the steps, in order, in a series of boxes.

    Main Idea and Details Chart   This graphic organizer may be used with a variety of writing assignments. Students write a main idea in one box and the details that support it in another box.

    Two-Column Chart   This graphic organizer can be used with a variety of writing tasks. Students could use the chart to write a main idea in one column and the details that support it in the other column. They could also use the chart's two columns to compare and contrast, to list problems and solutions, or causes and effects.

  ### Word and Definition Cards
  Word cards for each target vocabulary word as well as cards with the definitions for the words are on pages 99–128 of this Teacher Guide. You may either cut the cards out of the book or photocopy them, cut them apart, and then use them. For ideas on how to use the word and definition cards, see page 10 of this Teacher Guide.

  ### Take-Home Activities
  Each student book lesson has a take-home activity for additional practice and an opportunity for students to share what they have learned with family members.

Vocabulary Teaching Strategies

These teaching strategies have been shown to be effective with English language learners, but all students who are studying vocabulary will find them helpful.

Accessing Prior Knowledge

Like their English-speaking peers, English language learners come to the classroom with a large body of knowledge. The challenge as a teacher of English language learners is tapping into this knowledge. Before introducing a lesson topic, ask students what they already know about the subject. By doing this, you not only acknowledge students' experiences, but you also find out what information and misinformation students have about the topic. This will enable you to plan a more relevant and focused lesson. Each student book lesson of ***Passwords: Social Studies Vocabulary*** begins with an introductory paragraph written to tap into students' prior knowledge and to provide motivation for reading. In addition, this Teacher Guide includes a prior knowledge activity for each lesson.

Picture File

Use magazines or Web sources to create a file of pictures for selected social studies topics. Students will enjoy looking for pictures and pasting them on construction paper. Use the pictures to illustrate target vocabulary words or key concepts. Pictures can be used before, during, or after reading in matching games, gallery walks, and as writing prompts.

Graphic Organizers

This Teacher Guide includes four vocabulary graphic organizers and four writing graphic organizers that can be reproduced for use by students. (See pages 76–83.)

Vocabulary graphic organizers can provide students with a visual representation of a word's meaning by showing examples, synonyms, drawings, descriptions, or the definition of the word. Students can add to the graphic organizer as their understanding of the word increases.

Writing graphic organizers help students organize their thoughts and plan their writing. The writing graphic organizers included in this Teacher Guide are intended for use with different kinds of Write! activities.

Total Physical Response

Total Physical Response, or TPR, is a language-teaching method first developed by Dr. James Asher, a professor of psychology. Asher based his method on his observations of how children learn their native language. In TPR, teachers replace parents, modeling verbal commands, while students respond physically. As a language-teaching method, TPR emphasizes listening and physical response over written language. It has been found to be an effective method for teaching vocabulary. In using TPR to teach vocabulary, teachers and students use movement to associate a word with its meaning. For example, to teach the target vocabulary word *ally*, have your students stand up and link their arms. To teach the word *isolationism*, have students move their desks in tight, separate clusters. To use TPR in your classroom, give commands that require a physical response from students. When they are ready, students can reverse roles, giving commands to you and to fellow students.

Context Clues

Students need to be directly instructed on how to use context clues to help them figure out the meaning of unknown words. There are several different kinds of context clues.

- **Definition**
  In this type of context clue, a definition, or restatement, of the unknown word is provided in the text. Words that signal a definition context clue include *means, refers to,* or *is*. Definition context clues are frequently used in ***Passwords: Social Studies Vocabulary***.

- **Synonym**
  Writers sometimes use familiar words with similar meanings to build meaning for an unknown or unfamiliar word.

- **Example**
  Point out that writers will sometimes provide an example for students that will help them figure out the meaning of an unfamiliar word. Words that may signal an example include *like, these, for example,* and *such as.*

Cognates

Cognates are words in different languages that resemble one another in both sound and meaning. Spanish and English have many cognates, especially in the area of social studies where words in both languages draw upon Latin and Greek roots. Some cognates are spelled identically, although pronunciation differs; for example the words *capital, tractor,* and *radio*. Others are spelled similarly; *cultura* and *culture*. Other words that seem similar are not cognates at all. *Bigote* does not mean "bigot"; it means "mustache."

Teachers cannot assume that Spanish-speaking students will automatically or correctly connect an English word with a Spanish cognate. To help students develop the ability to recognize cognates, each ***Passwords: Social Studies Vocabulary*** Teacher Guide lesson includes a list of the Spanish cognates for the target vocabulary in that lesson. As you discuss these cognates with students, point out spelling patterns, such as *-tion* (English) and *-ción* (Spanish). This will help students develop generalizations about language patterns and enhance their ability to use their knowledge of their native language to learn English. Encourage your Spanish-speaking students to guess at the meaning of words in English based on their knowledge of Spanish. If you read the selections aloud, ask Spanish speakers to indicate when they think they hear a cognate. If students read the selections themselves, have them write down the words they think might be cognates. Discuss possible cognates when students have finished reading the selection. Write the word pairs on the board and have students come to the board and circle the similarities between the two words. Have students look for patterns. Students who speak languages other than Spanish may also be able to find English cognates of words from their native languages.

Greek and Latin Roots

Introducing the study of Greek and Latin roots to students who are learning English may initially seem to be adding another layer of difficulty to language learning. However, students who speak a Romance language (Spanish, French, Italian, Portuguese, Romanian) will often find that the Latin or Greek root of an English word is similar to a word they know in their own language. Students who speak Haitian Creole may find that their native language, which draws heavily upon French, also has many links to Latin.

When teaching students how to use roots to determine word meaning, remind them that many long English words are made up of smaller parts. The root of the word is the part that contains the most important aspect of the word's meaning. For example, if students come across the word *territory* and they recognize the root *terra* from their study of Greek and Latin roots and they remember that the root *terra* is related to land, they can begin to figure out that *territory* has something to do with land.

Students will find a chart of Greek and Latin roots, with examples of target vocabulary words that have those roots, on page 99 of the student book.

Prefixes and Suffixes

A prefix is a word part that is attached to the beginning of a base word. A suffix is a word part that is attached to the end of a base word. The meaning of a prefix or suffix combines with the meaning of the base word. For example, the prefix *in-*, meaning "not," combines with *dependence* to form *independence*, "not dependent." The suffix *-ion*, meaning "the action of," combines with *industrial* to form a noun, *industrialization*. Knowing the meaning of common prefixes and suffixes is another tool students can use to help them figure out the meaning of unknown words and remember the meaning of words they are learning. Students will find a chart of common prefixes and suffixes, with examples of target vocabulary words that have these prefixes or suffixes, on page 100 of the student book.

Word Cards

This Teacher Guide includes reproducible word and definition cards on pages 99–128. Each page contains one lesson's words or definitions. These cards can be used in teacher-led activities, and small group activities, to introduce new vocabulary, and to review vocabulary and concepts. Word cards are helpful to visual, kinesthetic, and aural learners. Word cards provide students with visual cues and constant reinforcement. Many word card activities require you to create copies of the cards. You can photocopy the cards on cardstock or on plain paper. If you want to use the cards as flashcards, with the definition on the back, photocopy the pages as two-sided copies.

For many activities, however, you will need cards with one blank side and the word or the definition on the other side. After you make the copies, cut the cards apart. Store the cards in labeled plastic zipper bags with a set of cards, you might consider having students create their own cards using blank 3½" × 5" file cards. Although you will certainly come up with many ideas of how to use these cards on your own, here are a few activities to begin with.

- ## Word Wall

  A Word Wall can be a great tool in helping students learn vocabulary. Although words are generally displayed on a bulletin board, you can also use more portable display surfaces, such as a shower curtain or a trifold board. Add words to the Word Wall as you introduce the target vocabulary. Review the words daily. Change the words as you begin a new lesson. Word Walls lend themselves to a variety of activities.

  ### Five Clues

  Have each student number their paper from one to five. Give a clue about one of the words on the Word Wall. Students should write down the word they think you are thinking of. Keep giving clues (up to five) until everyone has guessed the word you were thinking of.

  ### Lights On!

  You'll need a flashlight for this activity. Turn off the classroom lights. Then point the flashlight at one word on the Word Wall. Call on a student to read the word and either use it in a sentence or provide the definition. When the student is successful, it is his or her turn to point the flashlight at a word and choose another student to read the word.

  ### Wordo

  Provide each student with a bingo-type grid with six blank spaces. Tell students to fill in the blanks with words from the Word Wall. Put the corresponding definition cards into a jar. Pull the definition cards from the jar one by one. Read the definition and have students cover the corresponding word on their grid with a marker. When the entire card is covered, Wordo!

- ## Card Games

  The word cards can be used in many different card games, some of which are variations of games played with regular playing cards. Here are a few ideas for games using the word cards.

  ### Concentration

  The object of this game is to find matching pairs. Prepare two sets of cards. One set of cards has the target vocabulary words and the other set has the definitions. Prepare from 10 cards (for 5 matches) to 30 cards (15 matches). Mix up the two sets of cards. Place the cards face down in rows. Players take turns turning over pairs of cards. If the cards match, the player makes a sentence using the vocabulary word. If the cards don't match, play goes to the next player. If the student successfully creates a sentence using the vocabulary word, he or she goes again. The player with the most cards at the end is the winner.

  ### Guess the Word

  This game is for four students, playing in pairs. Prepare a card for each target vocabulary word. Put the cards face down in the middle of the table. The first student of the first pair picks a card and gives a one-word clue to his or her partner that will enable the partner to guess the vocabulary word. If the partner does not guess the word, the word goes to a member of the other pair who gives a hint to his or her partner. The team that successfully guesses the word keeps the card. The team with the most cards wins.

What Is the Need for *Passwords: Social Studies Vocabulary?*

Learning academic vocabulary is essential to each student's comprehension of content-area materials. Researchers (Bailey, 2007; Resnick, 2006; Ogle, Klemp, & McBride, 2007; Yarbrough, 2007) have shown that many content-area texts may present learning barriers to students. In a 2006 textbook survey by Education Market Research, teachers were asked about the biggest problems they experienced with their current text. Teachers stated that texts that are "hard for students to read" (35.2%) was the biggest problem, followed closely by "doesn't meet needs of diverse students" (31.4%). Several factors may make a text hard to read, such as:

- A textbook analysis found that some texts are written approximately 2 to 4 reading levels above grade level. This fact highlights why students may struggle with content-area instructional materials (Yarbrough, 2007).

- Social studies texts are more lexically dense and the wording of these texts are not typical to what students hear and say in everyday life (Bailey, 2007).

- Background knowledge of a topic may not be incorporated into a new lesson, causing a disconnect for students who are not familiar with a specific social-studies topic (Ogle, Klemp, & McBride, 2007).

- Struggling readers have difficulty with nonlinear reading. Excess use of photographs, charts, maps, and graphs can inhibit rather than support a struggling reader's comprehension (Ogle, Klemp, & McBride, 2007).

Concerns about students' comprehension of content-area texts continues to grow. The 2006 National Assessment of Educational Progress (NAEP) Social Studies Assessment reported minor increases in the "Basic" level of performance of 4th- and 8th-grade students (Lee & Weiss, 2007). While these results are encouraging, the reauthorization of the No Child Left Behind Act (NCLB) proposes to make NAEP results even more significant. Under the NCLB reauthorization, NAEP assessment scores will be listed alongside each state's scores. This comparison of scores is meant to close the achievement gap between state tests and the NAEP tests (U.S. Department of Ed., 2007). This new initiative heightens the need for students to master academic vocabulary for better comprehension of content-area materials.

Passwords: Social Studies Vocabulary is a tool that can support students who struggle with "hard-to-read" texts. It unites students with a singular goal of successfully learning the academic language of social studies. This goal is attainable through the instructional features and strategies that research has proven to be effective with diverse student populations.

Why Is *Passwords: Social Studies Vocabulary* Helpful to ELL Students?

Academic language proficiency is the ability of the student to comprehend, speak, read, and write when the context is reduced and the topic is cognitively demanding. Examples of cognitively demanding activities are reading textbooks, writing long compositions, learning new concepts, and mastering local and state requirements that test students on the academic language of each content area. Zelasko & Antunez (2000) state that "without mastery of classroom English, they [ELL students] will have difficulty competing academically in an all-English setting." The importance of learning academic language is confirmed by additional researchers (August, Carlo, Dressler, & Snow, 2005):

- "Vocabulary development is one of the greatest challenges to reading instruction for ELLs, because in order to read fluently and comprehend what is written, students need to use not just phonics, but context" (Antunez, 2002).

- "For English language learners, academic English is like a third language, their second language being the social English of the hallways, community, and media. And whereas students are exposed to social English in various settings, academic language acquisition is generally limited to the classroom. . . . Many English language learners, even those with well-developed social language, struggle to master the complex language of school" (Zwiers, 2004/2005).

What Are the Strategies and Features in *Passwords: Social Studies Vocabulary* that Research Has Proven to Be Effective with ELL Students?

Social studies is a cognitively demanding school subject. In addition, the vocabulary of social studies is also considered as Tier III vocabulary, which requires direct and explicit instruction (Beck, McKeown, & Kucan, 2002). This is especially important for ELL students. The first step to comprehending the content of a school subject is to understand the vocabulary and language of the school subject. ***Passwords: Social Studies Vocabulary*** incorporates ELL instructional recommendations from content-area experts for teaching vocabulary.

Marzano & Pickering (2005), in *Building Academic Vocabulary*, promote a six-step process for teaching new terms. This process is also integrated in ***Passwords: Social Studies Vocabulary***.

Step 1: Provide a description, an explanation, or an example of the new term (along with a nonlinguistic representation).

Step 2: Ask students to restate the description, explanation, or example in their own words.

Step 3: Ask students to construct a picture, symbol, or graphic representing the term.

Step 4: Engage students periodically in activities that help them add to their knowledge of the terms.

Step 5: Engage students periodically to discuss the terms with one another.

Step 6: Involve students periodically in games that allow them to play with terms.

Additionally, educational experts and researchers from numerous professional organizations (Association for Supervision and Curriculum Developers, English Language Summit, and International Reading Association) have created a list of instructional recommendations that have been found to be effective, especially with ELL students. While these organizations are separate entities, they share some common recommendations. These recommendations are integrated throughout ***Passwords: Social Studies Vocabulary***.

Passwords: Social Studies Vocabulary Uses . . .	Research Says . . .
Direct Instruction Within Context (SB, Reading Selection & Activities A–D)	*"The teaching of individual words is most effective when learners are given both definitional and contextual information, when learners actively process the new word meanings, and when they experience multiple encounters with words"* (Graves & Watts-Taffe, 2002).
Prior-Knowledge Activation (SB, Prereading Activity; TG)	*"To facilitate communication of content knowledge, teachers can offer support in several ways: Plan adequate time to activate students' prior knowledge and encourage students to share what they already know in journals, small groups, or paired brainstorming sessions"* (Rolón, 2002/2003).
Collaborative Learning (SB, Prereading Activity & Activities A–D; TG)	*"Students interacting verbally with other native speakers of English pick up vocabulary and content knowledge"* (Association of American Publishers, 2004). *"Research and common sense . . . confirm that interacting with other people about what we are learning deepens the understanding of everyone involved—particularly when we are learning new terms"* (Marzano & Pickering, 2005).
Differentiated Instruction (SB, Activities A–D; TG)	*"Numerous theorists and contemporary translators of brain research propose that students do not learn effectively when tasks are too simple or too complex for their particular readiness levels. Rather, say these researchers, tasks must be moderately challenging for the individual for growth to occur"* (Tomlinson, 2004).
Parental Engagement (TG, Take-Home Activities)	*"The evidence is consistent, positive, and convincing: families have a major influence on their children's achievement in school and through life"* (Henderson & Mapp, 2002).
Total Physical Response (TG, Vocabulary Teaching Strategies section, During Reading Activity)	*"Having children physically act out songs, poems, or readings—all forms of TPR methodology—is an effective way to support vocabulary development"* (Drucker, 2003). In a research synthesis, Slavin & Cheung (2005) state that teachers of English language learners may use language development strategies, such as total physical response, to help students internalize new vocabulary.

(Continues)

Passwords: Social Studies Vocabulary Uses . . .	Research Says . . .
Considerate Text (SB, Reading Selections)	*"Certain features of text make it more 'considerate,' or easier to read and understand. The features should have clear concepts, consistent text structure, references that are easy to locate, and vocabulary that is precise and relates clearly to the subject. . . . A considerate text makes comprehension easier" (Dyck & Pemberton, 2002).*
Graphic Organizers (Semantic Feature Analysis & Semantic Mapping) (TG, Pre- & Post-reading Activities)	*Hedrick, Harmon, & Linerode (2004, 2000) have analyzed content-area textbooks and have concluded that "textbooks infrequently include visual representations of concepts as a vocabulary instructional strategy."*
Clear and Explicit Illustrations and Artwork (SB, Reading Selections)	*"Giving an ESL student a nonlinguistic representation will provide a way for them to understand the meaning of the term that is not dependent on an understanding of English" (Marzano & Pickering, 2005).*
Deep Word-Study Activities (Roots, Prefixes, Suffixes, Cognates) (SB/TG)	*Students may find learning English easier if there are similar roots and pre/suffixes between their first language and English. Hansen (2006) suggests exploring cognates in order to aid students in making connections between their first language and English.* *"Teaching a word's facets of meaning moves students beyond a narrow definition of a word" (Beck, McKeown, & Kucan, 2002).*
Word Play Activities (TG, Take-Home Activities, Word Cards)	*Researchers (Marzano & Pickering, 2005; Paynter, Bodrova, & Doty, 2005; Richek, 2005) stress that word play builds a strong connection to newly learned vocabulary.* *"Activities using words in games, connecting words, and manipulating words creatively result in excellent student learning" (Beck, McKeown, & Kucan, 2002).*
Association/ Connection Methods: (Personal Connection, Picture Connection, Word Connection) (SB/TG, throughout each lesson, Glossary)	*"This step is particularly important to ESL students. Whereas they might be constrained in their ability to devise a linguistic description, explanation, or example, they will not be constrained in their ability to create a nonlinguistic representation . . . These representations will most likely reflect the students' native culture, which is exactly the intent. Learning academic terms involves making connections with things familiar to us, and these things commonly arise from experiences native to our culture" (Marzano & Pickering, 2005).*
Modeling Through Audio (Passwords Audio CD)	*"When English language learners can simultaneously hear and read content-related information . . . it helps them decipher the text structures commonly found in textbooks" (Rubinstein-Ávila, 2006).*
Read Alouds (TG)	*"Teacher read-alouds are perhaps the most consistent activity used by classroom teachers that provides frequent, if not daily, opportunities to enhance the literacy of ELLs by integrating effective vocabulary development practices" (Hickman, Pollard-Durodola, & Vaughn, 2004).*
Speaking, Listening, Reading, Writing Experiences (SB/TG, throughout each lesson)	*"Successful word learning is active. Students learn words by using them. Thinking, saying, and writing new words help us make new words our own" (Bromley, 2003).* *García (1999) recommended that teachers use ". . . curriculum materials that are rich in opportunities for speaking, listening, reading, and writing in English."*

References

Antunez, B. (2002). English language learners and the five essential components of reading comprehension. Accessed February 27, 2006, from http://www.readingrockets.org/articles/341#vocab.

Association of American Publishers. (Fall 2004). English Language Learners summit proceedings, AAP School Division. Summit on English Language Learners. The Washington Court Hotel, Washington, DC. October 12, 2004. Accessed January 16, 2006, from http://www.publishers.org/SchoolDiv/research/research_03/research_03_Rep_05.htm.

August, D., Carlo, M., Dressler, C., & Snow, C. (2005). The critical role of vocabulary development for English language learners. *Learning Disabilities Research & Practice, 20*(1), 50–57.

Bailey, A. L. (Ed.). (2007). *The language demands of school: Putting academic English to the test.* New Haven: Yale University Press.

Beck, I. L., McKeown, M. G., & Kucan, L. (2002). *Bringing words to life: Robust vocabulary instruction.* New York: Guilford Press.

Bromley, K. (2003, April). Vocabulary S-t-r-e-t-c-h-e-r-s, *Instructor, 112*(7).

Drucker, M. J. (2003). What reading teachers should know about ESL learners: Good teaching is teaching for all. *The Reading Teacher, 57*(1).

Dyck, N., & Pemberton, J. B. (2002). A model for making decisions about text adaptations. *Intervention in School & Clinic, 38*(1).

García, E. (1999). *Student cultural diversity: Understanding and meeting the challenge* (2nd ed.). Boston: Houghton Mifflin.

Graves, M. F., & Watts-Taffe, S. M. (2002). The place of word consciousness in a research-based vocabulary program in *What research has to say about reading instruction.* Newark, DE: International Reading Association.

Hedrick, W. B., Harmon, J. M., & Linerode, P. M. (2004). Teachers' beliefs and practices of vocabulary instruction with social studies textbooks in Grades 4–8. *Reading Horizons, 45*(2), 103–125.

Hedrick, W. B., Harmon, J. M., & Linerode, P. M. (2000). Content analysis of vocabulary instruction in social studies textbooks for grades 4–8. *Elementary School Journal, 100*(3), 253–271.

Henderson, A. T., & Mapp, K. L. (2002). *A new wave of evidence: The impact of school, family, and community connections on student achievement. Annual Synthesis 2002.* National Center for Family & Community Connections with Schools. Austin: Southwest Educational Development Laboratory.

Hickman, P., Pollard-Durodola, S., & Vaughn, S. (2004). Storybook reading: Improving vocabulary and comprehension for English-language learners. *Reading Teacher, 57*(8), 720–730.

Lee, J., & Weiss, A. (2007). *The Nation's Report Card: U.S. History 2006* (NCES 2007–474). U.S. Department of Education, National Center for Education Statistics. Washington, DC: U.S. Government Printing Office.

Marzano, R. J., & Pickering, D. J. (2005). *Building Academic Vocabulary: Teacher's manual.* Alexandria, VA: ASCD.

Ogle, D., Klemp, R., & McBride, B. (2007). *Building literacy in social studies: Strategies for improving comprehension and critical thinking.* Washington, DC: Association for Supervision and Curriculum Development.

Paynter, D. E., Bodrova, E., & Doty, J. K. (2005). *For the love of words: Vocabulary instruction that works, grades K–6.* San Francisco: Jossey Bass.

Resnick, B. (2006). Social studies market, Grades K–12. Rockaway Park, NY: Education Market Research.

Richek, M. A. (2005, February). Words are wonderful: Interactive, time-efficient strategies to teach meaning vocabulary. *Reading Teacher, 58*(5), 414–423.

Rolón, C. A. (2002/2003). Educating Latino students. *Educational Leadership, 60*(4), 40–3.

Rubinstein-Ávila, E. (2006). Connecting with Latino Learners. *Educational Leadership, 63*(5), 38–43.

Slavin, R. E., & Cheung, A. (2005). Synthesis of research on language of reading instruction for English language learners. *Review of Educational Research Summer, 75*(2), 247–284.

Tomlinson, C. A. (2004, April). Differentiation in diverse settings. *School Administrator, 61*(7).

U.S. Department of Education. (2004). *Parental involvement: Title One, Part A Non-regulatory guidance.* Washington, DC: No Child Left Behind.

U.S. Department of Education, *Building on Results: A Blueprint for Strengthening the No Child Left Behind Act,* Washington, DC, 2007.

Yarbrough, B. (2007). Why Johnny Can't Read His Textbook. *Hesperia Star.* Accessed April 25, 2007, from http://www.hesperiastar.com/onset?id=656&template=article.html.

Zelasko, N., & Antunez, B. (2000). *If your child learns in two languages: A parent's guide for improving educational opportunities for children acquiring English as a second language.* National Clearinghouse of Bilingual Education: The George Washington University: Graduate School of Education and Human Development. Washington, DC.

Zwiers, J. (2004/2005). The third language of academic English. *Educational Leadership, 62*(4), 60–63.

LESSON 1

The Break from Great Britain

(Student Book pages 4–9)

Lesson Summary The early 1700s were a time of change in the American colonies. The Great Awakening in religion lead colonists to have renewed trust in their own political ideas. By 1770, many colonists wanted independence from Great Britain and in 1775, the American Revolution began. Thomas Jefferson wrote the Declaration of Independence in which he outlined the colonists' reasons for desiring their independence. In 1783, the war ended. The United States of America was a free and independent nation.

TARGET VOCABULARY

colony an area ruled by another country

preach talk about religious ideas

Great Awakening a period of renewed interest in religion

authority official power

political having to do with the government

independence freedom

revolution a war against one's own government

declaration serious statement about something

rights freedoms that are protected by law

clause a section of a piece of writing

COGNATES

Spanish-speaking students may find a discussion of the similarities and differences between English and Spanish cognates helpful.

English	Spanish
colony	colonia
authority	autoridad
political	político
independence	independencia
revolution	revolución
declaration	declaración
clause	cláusula

BEFORE READING

Activate Prior Knowledge

Discuss with students why a country would not want to be ruled by another country that is far away. Ask students what they know about why the United States wanted to break away from Great Britain in the 1700s. Write their ideas on the board. Return to students' ideas as they complete the lesson. Have them compare their ideas with what they have learned in the lesson.

Introduce Target Vocabulary

Tell students that they are about to read a selection about the 13 colonies' break with Great Britain. Write the target vocabulary words on the board. Model the pronunciation of each word and have student volunteers repeat the word. Discuss the meaning of each word and, if necessary, write the definition next to the word.

Present Graphic Organizer

Provide each student with a copy of Vocabulary Graphic Organizer: Word Chart, Teacher Guide page 76. Have students choose or assign each student a target vocabulary word. Direct students to write their word in the first box. As they read the selection, students should fill in the other boxes.

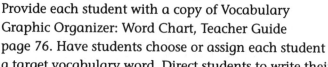
Word and Definition Cards for Lesson 1 are on pages 99 and 100 of the Teacher Guide.

VOCABULARY STRATEGY: Print Features

Point out the words in bold type in the reading selection. Tell students that these are target vocabulary words. They are important words that students should focus on and be sure that they understand as they read. Point out how the target vocabulary words appear across the top of most of the pages in the students' books. Tell students that there are two ways to find the meaning of words in bold type. They can use context clues in the reading. These context clues usually appear right next to the word in bold type. They can also use the glossary in the back of their book to find meanings.

The Break from Great Britain

LESSON 1

colony	Great Awakening	political	revolution	rights
preach	authority	independence	declaration	clause

Religion has played an important part in American history. Some of the first English settlers came to America because of their beliefs. Read this selection to learn about another time when religion changed history.

The Break from Great Britain

The Great Awakening

In the early 1600s everyone in England was expected to join the Church of England. Some people were not happy with the Church's rules. Some left England and came to North America. Some settled in colonies in New England. A **colony** is an area ruled by another country. Over time, however, religion became less important to people in the colonies.

Then, in the 1730s, people became interested in religion again. Men like Jonathan Edwards began to **preach**, or talk about religious subjects, in an exciting way. New churches with new ideas sprang up. This time is known as the **Great Awakening**.

People returned to church during the Great Awakening.

Colonists developed new religious ideas. They put less trust in religious authority. **Authority** is official power. Soon, they put less trust in political authority. **Political** means having to do with the government. The Great Awakening helped bring about the American Revolution.

The Declaration of Independence and the American Revolution

By 1770, many colonists wanted **independence**, or freedom, from Great Britain. In 1775, battles broke out between the colonists and British soldiers. The American Revolution had begun. A **revolution** is a war against one's own government.

British soldiers fired on an angry crowd in Boston in 1770.

In 1776, Thomas Jefferson and other leaders met in Philadelphia. They wanted to declare their freedom from Great Britain. Jefferson wrote a **declaration**, a serious statement about something. In the Declaration of Independence, Jefferson wrote that all people are born with rights. **Rights** are freedoms that are protected by law. The Declaration of Independence states that government should protect the rights of the people.

Jefferson also included a **clause**, or section, ending the slave trade. Some people refused to approve this clause. Jefferson was forced to remove it. On July 4, 1776, the Declaration of Independence was approved. The colonies stated that they were free. Their war for freedom would last seven more years.

In 1783, the American Revolution ended. The United States of America was a free country. It was now time to form a new government.

The Declaration of Independence says that all men are created equal.

My Social Studies Vocabulary
Go to page 94 to list other words you have learned about the break from Great Britain.

DURING READING

Read the selection aloud to students, as they follow along in their books. Pause at the end of each paragraph or section to review any words of concepts that students are having trouble understanding. Remind students that there is a glossary at the back of their book that contains all of the words that appear in boldfaced type in the lesson.

- Tell students that *colony* comes from the Latin word *colere*, meaning "to grow." Have them examine other words from the same root, such as *agriculture*, *cultivate*, and *culture*, and draw conclusions about how *colony* may be connected to the root meaning. (*Setting up colonies was one way to "grow" the land holdings of a country.*)

- Direct students' attention to the illustration of the Boston Massacre on page 5. Point out that the picture is not an accurate representation of what happened. It was created to turn people against the British. Students may be interested to know that Paul Revere, the famous patriot, created this engraving.

- Ask students if they can think of another word that sounds the same as *clause* but is spelled differently (*claws*). Tell students that words that are spelled differently but sound the same are homophones. Ask students to name other homophones. Some common homophones students may know are *bear* and *bare*, *their* and *there*, *eye* and *I*, and *right* and *write*.

Have students read the selection again on their own.

AFTER READING

Review Graphic Organizer

Answer any questions students have about the reading selection. Then have students complete or review their graphic organizer and share it with the class.

Summarize

Have students work together to come up with either a written or an oral summary of the lesson. Encourage students to use the target vocabulary words as the basis of their summary. Have students share their summary with the class.

My Social Studies Vocabulary

Encourage students to turn to My Social Studies Vocabulary on page 94 of the student book and use the space provided to add other words about the break from Great Britain.

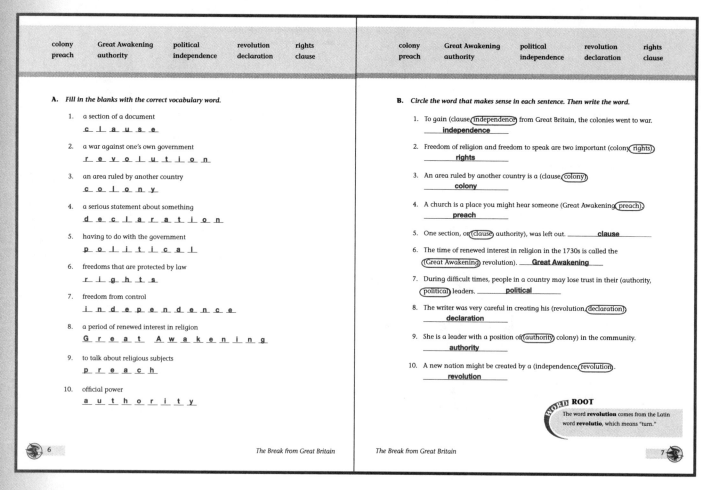

ACTIVITIES A–D

Encourage students to complete as many of the activities as possible. Remind students that they may refer to the Glossary at the back of their book as they complete the activities. Students may work independently, in small groups, or as a class. When students are done, discuss the answers for each activity.

Extensions

These extension ideas allow you to reuse or expand upon the activities. Share them with students who complete the activities before other students, or have students do them for additional practice with target vocabulary words.

A Rearrange the target vocabulary words so that they are in alphabetical order.

B Explain why the other word does not make sense in the sentence.

C Write the number of syllables in each target vocabulary word.

D Choose one sentence you wrote and add two more sentences that provide more information about the topic or the target vocabulary word.

WORD ROOT

Break the word *revolution* into its prefix *re-* and its root *volver*. Remind students that *re-* means "back" or "again." Then have students brainstorm other words that might come from the Latin root *volver*, meaning "to turn." Students may mention *evolution* or *involve*.

C. *Choose the correct vocabulary word to complete each sentence.*

1. People became interested in religion again when they heard Jonathan Edwards _____**preach**_____ .

2. For many years, Virginia was a _____**colony**_____ under the rule of Great Britain.

3. The legal paper had a _____**clause**_____ , or section, that no one understood.

4. A government should protect the _____**rights**_____ of the people.

5. We choose _____**political**_____ leaders in elections.

6. New churches were formed during the _____**Great Awakening**_____ of the 1730s.

7. Choose your words carefully when you write a _____**declaration**_____ .

8. When people in positions of _____**authority**_____ speak, you should listen.

9. Americans fought for their _____**independence**_____ from Great Britain.

10. Many soldiers died in the long and bloody _____**revolution**_____ .

Students' answers will vary.

D. *Use each pair of words in a sentence.*

1. colony, independence

   The colony was willing to go to war for its independence.

2. preach, Great Awakening

   During the Great Awakening, people traveled far to hear Jonathan Edwards preach.

3. declaration, clause

   One clause of the declaration states that people should have a fair trial.

4. authority, political

   The president is an example of a political authority.

5. revolution, rights

   Would you fight in a revolution to get your rights?

Write!

Write your response to the prompt on a separate sheet of paper. Use as many vocabulary words as you can in your writing.

How did religion help shape American history in the early years of our country?

Write!

Provide each student with a copy of Writing Graphic Organizer: Topic Web, Teacher Guide page 80. Tell students to write "religion" in the top circle. In the lower circles they should write ways in which religion helped shape early American history.

Sample Answer

Many of the first people to settle in what is now the United States came because of religion. They hoped to find freedom to practice their religion in the colonies.

Over the years, religion became less important. Then in the 1730's, the Great Awakening sparked a new interest in religion. Jonathan Edwards and others preached in an exciting way. New religious ideas led to new political ideas. Soon colonists wanted freedom from old political authority as well as freedom from old religious authority. This renewed interest in religion would lead to the American Revolution.

TAKE-HOME ACTIVITY

Assign the Take-Home Activity to students for additional practice with the target vocabulary words. The reproducible Take-Home Activity for Lesson 1 is on page 84 of the Teacher Guide.

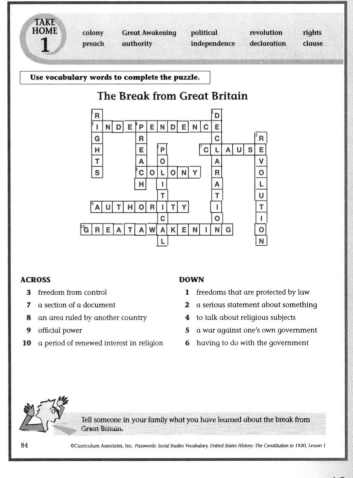

TAKE HOME 1

colony	Great Awakening	political	revolution	rights
preach	authority	independence	declaration	clause

Use vocabulary words to complete the puzzle.

The Break from Great Britain

ACROSS

3 freedom from control
7 a section of a document
8 an area ruled by another country
9 official power
10 a period of renewed interest in religion

DOWN

1 freedoms that are protected by law
2 a serious statement about something
4 to talk about religious subjects
5 a war against one's own government
6 having to do with the government

Tell someone in your family what you have learned about the break from Great Britain.

84   ©Curriculum Associates, Inc. *Passwords: Social Studies Vocabulary, United States History: The Constitution to 1920, Lesson 1*

LESSON 2

The Roots of the Constitution

(Student Book pages 10–15)

Lesson Summary The Magna Carta, signed by the king of England in 1215, is one document that shaped our Constitution. The Magna Carta limited the power of the king. It set up a parliament that would make laws. In 1689, the English Bill of Rights decreed that the monarch was subject to the laws passed by Parliament and that Parliament had the right to set and collect taxes. In the colonies, the *Mayflower Compact* was another stone in the Constitution's foundation.

TARGET VOCABULARY

constitution a set of laws and ideas that describe how a government works

foundation the base upon which something is built

Magna Carta a list of rights signed by the king of England in 1215

parliament a group of people chosen to make laws

document a formal piece of writing

subject under the power of another

taxation the system of paying taxes, or money paid to support the government

monarchy a country ruled by one person

pilgrim a person who makes a long trip for religious reasons

compact an agreement

COGNATES

Spanish-speaking students may find a discussion of the similarities and differences between English and Spanish cognates helpful.

English	Spanish
constitution	constitución
foundation	fundamento
parliament	parlamento
document	documento
monarchy	monarquía

BEFORE READING

Activate Prior Knowledge
Develop a word web on the board with student volunteers suggesting words to surround the word *constitution*. Ask students which details might have been most important to the founders of our nation.

Introduce Target Vocabulary
Tell students that they are about to read a selection about the roots of the Constitution. Write the target vocabulary words on the board. Model the pronunciation of each word and have student volunteers repeat the word. Discuss the meaning of each word and, if necessary, write the definition next to the word.

Present Graphic Organizer
Provide each student with a copy of Vocabulary Graphic Organizer: Vocabulary Map, Teacher Guide page 77. Have each student choose a target vocabulary word or assign a target word to each student. As students read, they should add information about the target vocabulary word to the graphic organizer.

> Word and Definition Cards
> for Lesson 2 are on pages 101 and 102
> of the Teacher Guide.

VOCABULARY STRATEGY: Context Clues

Remind students to use context clues to find the meanings of unfamiliar words. Explain that some context clues are definition clues. Direct students' attention to the first sentence of the reading selection. Have students find the word *constitution* and its definition. Point out how the definition for *constitution* directly follows the word *is*. Explain that *is* often signals a definition clue, and have students write an equal sign above it. Then have them underline the definition that follows *is*. Have students find other examples of definition clues that begin with *is* in the text (*foundation, Magna Carta, taxation, pilgrim, compact*).

The reproduced student book page:

LESSON 2

| constitution | Magna Carta | document | taxation | pilgrim |
| foundation | parliament | subject | monarchy | compact |

A strong plant needs strong roots. A strong government needs strong roots too. What were the roots, or beginnings, of American government? Read this selection to find out.

The Roots of the Constitution

A **constitution** is a set of laws and ideas that describe how a government works. The United States Constitution describes the government of the United States. The United States Constitution was written in 1787. The foundation of our Constitution is much older. A **foundation** is the base upon which something is built. What forms the foundation of the Constitution?

The Magna Carta

In 1215 in England, a group of nobles met and wrote the Magna Carta. The **Magna Carta** is a list of political rights. Political rights are rights that have to do with the government. The Magna Carta set up a **parliament**, a group of people chosen to make laws. The English nobles forced the king to agree to it. The Magna Carta limited the power of the king.

King John is forced to agree to the Magna Carta.

The English Bill of Rights

In 1689, another historic **document**, or formal piece of writing, was created in England. This document is known as the Bill of Rights. In the English Bill of Rights, the king and queen of England agreed that they were **subject** to law. That means that the king and queen had to follow the laws that Parliament passed.

The English Bill of Rights also gave Parliament the right of taxation. **Taxation** is the system of paying taxes, or money paid to support the government. The English Bill of Rights limited the power of the monarchy. In a **monarchy**, a country is ruled by one person, such as a king or queen.

King William III and Queen Mary II are shown holding the English Bill of Rights.

The Mayflower Compact

Another document that shaped the Constitution was written in the Atlantic Ocean! In 1620, a group of people set sail across the Atlantic Ocean. The name of their ship was the *Mayflower*. They planned to start a new colony in North America. They called themselves the Pilgrims. A **pilgrim** is a person who makes a long trip for religious reasons. The Pilgrims came to America looking for religious freedom.

Before they landed, the Pilgrims wrote a plan for government. They called their plan the Mayflower Compact. A **compact** is an agreement. In the Mayflower Compact, the Pilgrims agreed to make laws for the good of the community. They also agreed to obey the laws of the colony.

A Pilgrim signs the Mayflower Compact.

 My Social Studies Vocabulary
Go to page 94 to list other words you have learned about the roots of the Constitution.

10   The Roots of the Constitution

The Roots of the Constitution   11

DURING READING

Read the selection aloud to students, as they follow along in their books. Pause at the end of each paragraph or section to review any words of concepts that students are having trouble understanding. Remind students that there is a glossary at the back of their book that contains all of the words that appear in boldfaced type in the lesson.

- Point out to students the difference between a common noun (*constitution, pilgrim*) and a proper noun (*the United States Constitution, Pilgrim*). Tell students that common nouns that refer to things in general are written with a small letter while words for specific things or people begin with capital letters.

- Tell students that *Magna Carta* is Latin for "great charter." A *charter* is a document that gives rights to people. Tell students that the Magna Carta, although an English document, was written, like most important papers of the time, in Latin.

- Students are probably with familiar with the word *subject* as a noun meaning, "something that is thought about" or "a course of study." Point out to students that in this lesson *subject* is an adjective and that it can also be used as a verb. Tell students that when used as a verb, *subject* is pronounced slightly differently. Have students create sentences using *subject* as an adjective, a noun, and a verb.

Have students read the selection again on their own.

AFTER READING

Review Graphic Organizer

Answer any questions students have about the reading selection. Then have students complete or review their graphic organizer and share it with the class.

Summarize

Have students work together to come up with either a written or an oral summary of the lesson. Encourage students to use the target vocabulary words as the basis of their summary. Have students share their summary with the class.

My Social Studies Vocabulary

Encourage students to turn to My Social Studies Vocabulary on page 94 of the student book and use the space provided to add other words about the roots of the Constitution.

The Roots of the Constitution

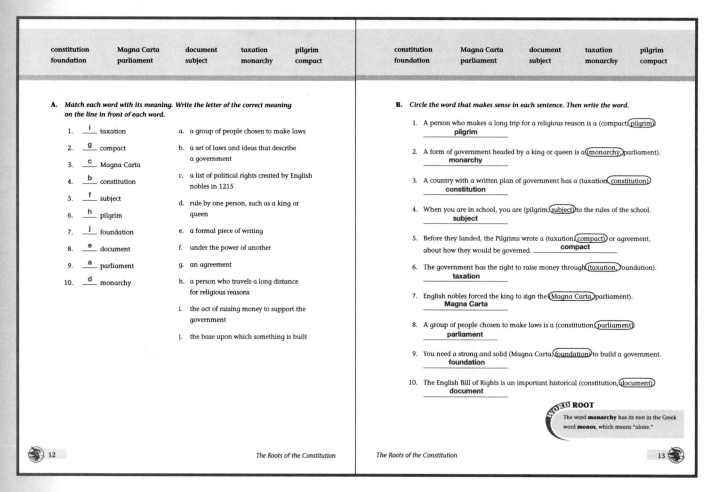

A. Match each word with its meaning. Write the letter of the correct meaning on the line in front of each word.

1. i taxation
2. g compact
3. c Magna Carta
4. b constitution
5. f subject
6. h pilgrim
7. j foundation
8. e document
9. a parliament
10. d monarchy

a. a group of people chosen to make laws
b. a set of laws and ideas that describe a government
c. a list of political rights created by English nobles in 1215
d. rule by one person, such as a king or queen
e. a formal piece of writing
f. under the power of another
g. an agreement
h. a person who travels a long distance for religious reasons
i. the act of raising money to support the government
j. the base upon which something is built

B. Circle the word that makes sense in each sentence. Then write the word.

1. A person who makes a long trip for a religious reason is a (compact, pilgrim). pilgrim
2. A form of government headed by a king or queen is a (monarchy, parliament). monarchy
3. A country with a written plan of government has a (taxation, constitution). constitution
4. When you are in school, you are (pilgrim, subject) to the rules of the school. subject
5. Before they landed, the Pilgrims wrote a (taxation, compact) or agreement, about how they would be governed. compact
6. The government has the right to raise money through (taxation, foundation). taxation
7. English nobles forced the king to sign the (Magna Carta, parliament). Magna Carta
8. A group of people chosen to make laws is a (constitution, parliament). parliament
9. You need a strong and solid (Magna Carta, foundation) to build a government. foundation
10. The English Bill of Rights is an important historical (constitution, document). document

WORD ROOT
The word **monarchy** has its root in the Greek word **monos**, which means "alone."

The Roots of the Constitution

ACTIVITIES A–D

Encourage students to complete as many of the activities as possible. Remind students that they may refer to the Glossary at the back of their book as they complete the activities. Students may work independently, in small groups, or as a class. When students are done, discuss the answers for each activity.

Extensions

These extension ideas allow you to reuse or expand upon the activities. Share them with students who complete the activities before other students, or have students do them for additional practice with target vocabulary words.

A Look up two of the target vocabulary words in the Glossary, in a dictionary, and in an encyclopedia. How are the definitions similar? How are they different?

B After you have chosen the correct answers for each sentence, explain why the wrong answers do not make sense in the sentence.

WORD ROOT

Discuss with students how the meaning of *monarchy* relates to its Greek root. (*In a monarchy, a king or queen rules alone.*) Tell students that another word for *king* or *queen* is *monarch*.

C Make a chart with three columns. Label the columns "Magna Carta," "English Bill of Rights," and "Mayflower Compact." Write the target vocabulary words under the correct heading. Some words belong in more than one column.

D Choose the hardest word on the list for you to define. Make up a memory device to help you remember what the word means.

The Roots of the Constitution

C. *Write the vocabulary word that best completes each pair of sentences.*

1. After the long trip, the _____**pilgrim**_____ entered the church to pray.
   The holy city welcomed each _____**pilgrim**_____ .

2. Some countries have a government, but do not have a _____**constitution**_____ .
   A written plan for government is called a _____**constitution**_____ .

3. The people who live in a country are _____**subject**_____ to its laws.
   Even kings and queens are _____**subject**_____ to the law.

4. A formal piece of writing is a _____**document**_____ .
   A report card is an example of a _____**document**_____ .

5. English nobles met with the king and made him sign the _____**Magna Carta**_____
   The power of the king was limited by the _____**Magna Carta**_____ .

6. According to our _____**compact**_____ , I wash the dishes and my brother
   dries them.
   Two nations may sign a _____**compact**_____ , or agreement to help
   each other.

7. For many years, the country was a _____**monarchy**_____ , ruled by a king.
   The power of a king or queen can be limited, even in a _____**monarchy**_____ .

8. It is difficult to build a nation without a solid _____**foundation**_____ .
   Like a building, a country needs a _____**foundation**_____ to build upon.

9. Countries raise money through _____**taxation**_____
   Governments need _____**taxation**_____ to pay for school and roads.

10. Laws are passed in the _____**parliament**_____ .
    How are members of _____**parliament**_____ chosen?

Students' answers will vary.
D. *Use each word in a sentence that shows you understand the meaning of the word.*

1. document **The Constitution is an important document.**

2. constitution **A constitution is a written plan of government.**

3. pilgrim **The pilgrim was happy to reach the holy site.**

4. subject **Students in school are subject to the rules of the school.**

5. foundation **The English Bill of Rights helped form the foundation of the United States Constitution.**

6. compact **In my compact with my mother, I clean my room, and she drives me to the mall.**

7. parliament **Parliament meets every year to pass new laws.**

8. taxation **Governments get money through taxation.**

9. monarchy **A king or queen would prefer to live in a monarchy.**

10. Magna Carta **The Magna Carta limited the power of the king.**

Write!
Write your response to the prompt on a separate sheet of paper.
Use as many vocabulary words as you can in your writing.

Choose one of the documents you read about. How, do you think, did that document serve as a foundation for the United States constitution?

Write! ✏️

Provide each student with a copy of Writing Graphic Organizer: Topic Web, Teacher Guide page 80. Tell students to write the name of the document they have chosen to write about in the center circle. In the other circles they should outline how that document serves as foundation for the United States Constitution.

Sample Answer

The English Bill of Rights served as a foundation for our own Constitution. Like the Magna Carta before it, the English Bill of Rights limited the power of the monarchy. In the English Bill of Rights, the rulers of England agreed they had to obey the laws. This is an idea that is also part of American law—that everyone must obey the law. The English Bill of Rights also said that Parliament has the power to collect taxes. In the United States, the government also has the power to collect taxes.

TAKE-HOME ACTIVITY 📖 ✏️ 🔄

Assign the Take-Home Activity to students for additional practice with the target vocabulary words. The reproducible Take-Home Activity for Lesson 2 is on page 85 of the Teacher Guide.

The Roots of the Constitution

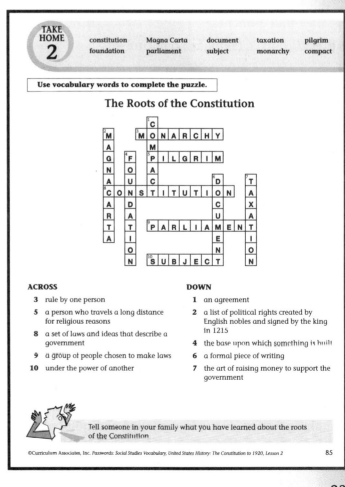

TAKE HOME 2

| constitution | Magna Carta | document | taxation | pilgrim |
| foundation | parliament | subject | monarchy | compact |

Use vocabulary words to complete the puzzle.

The Roots of the Constitution

ACROSS
3 rule by one person
5 a person who travels a long distance for religious reasons
8 a set of laws and ideas that describe a government
9 a group of people chosen to make laws
10 under the power of another

DOWN
1 an agreement
2 a list of political rights created by English nobles and signed by the king in 1215
4 the base upon which something is built
6 a formal piece of writing
7 the art of raising money to support the government

Tell someone in your family what you have learned about the roots of the Constitution

LESSON 3

The Constitution

(Student Book pages 16–21)

Lesson Summary The government created by the Articles of Confederation was weak. The new nation needed a stronger central government. In 1788, the United States Constitution was approved. The Constitution created a democracy under a system of federalism. The Congress created by the Constitution has two houses. Other hallmarks of the Constitution are its system of checks and balances, the separation of powers, and the reserved powers of the states.

TARGET VOCABULARY

confederation a group of independent states that work together

convention a meeting for a particular purpose

delegates people chosen to speak and vote for a group

compromise an agreement in which each side gives up something

democracy a government run by the people who live under it

federalism a system in which state and national governments share power and duties

reserved powers powers given to the states

separation of powers the separation of the government into three branches

checks and balances a system in which each branch of government can limit the actions of the other branches

amendment a change to a document

COGNATES

Spanish-speaking students may find a discussion of the similarities and differences between English and Spanish cognates helpful.

English	Spanish
confederation	confederación
convention	convención
democracy	democracia
federalism	federalismo
amendment	enmienda

VOCABULARY STRATEGY: Suffixes

Explain to students that some suffixes, letters added to the end of words, make a word a noun. These suffixes let you know that a word names a person, place, thing, or idea. Write these common noun-making suffixes found in the target vocabulary words: *-tion, -ion, -ment,* and *-ism.* Ask students to name the target vocabulary words that have these suffixes (*confederation, convention, federalism,* and *amendment*). Explain that all of these words are words that name things. Invite students to name other words they know with these suffixes and to explain why each is a naming word.

BEFORE READING

Activate Prior Knowledge

Give students a series of true/false questions like these:

- Federalism is the basis of the government of our country. *(true)*
- A convention is a big party. *(false)*
- A democracy is headed by a king. *(false)*

Have students compare their results and explain the reasons for their choices.

Introduce Target Vocabulary

Tell students they are about to read a selection about the Constitution. Write the target vocabulary words on the board. Model the pronunciation of each word and have student volunteers repeat the word. Discuss the meaning of each word and, if necessary, write the definition next to the word.

Present Graphic Organizer

Provide each student with a copy of Vocabulary Graphic Organizer: Four Square, Teacher Guide page 78. Have students choose or assign each student a target vocabulary word. As they read, students should add information about the vocabulary word to the graphic organizer.

> Word and Definition Cards for Lesson 3 are on pages 103 and 104 of the Teacher Guide.

The Constitution

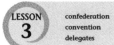

LESSON 3

confederation	compromise	reserved powers	checks and balances
convention	democracy	separation of powers	amendment
delegates	federalism		

How would you create a new form of government, one that no other country had? Read this selection to find out how the United States government was created.

The Constitution

The Articles of Confederation

In 1781, the original 13 states set up a national government. The Articles of Confederation laid out the new nation's government. A **confederation** is a group of independent states that work together. The first national government was weak. It had no leader or president. There were no courts to rule over all the states. The new government was not working. Changes had to be made.

The Constitutional Convention

In May 1787, the Constitutional Convention met in Philadelphia. A **convention** is a meeting for a particular purpose. **Delegates**, people chosen to speak and vote for a group, from 12 states were there. The delegates did not always agree.

George Washington was the leader of the Constitutional Convention.

States with many people thought they should have more power. States with fewer people wanted equal power. A compromise was made. In a **compromise**, each side gives up something to reach an agreement.

The Great Compromise

Plan A	Plan B
• Congress has two houses.	• Congress has one house.
• The number of representatives is based on population.	• Each state has the same number of representatives.

- Congress has two houses.
- In one house, the number of representatives is based on state population.
- In the other house, each state has the same number of representatives.

The Constitution

In 1788, the United States Constitution was approved. The Constitution created a **democracy**, a system of government run by the people who live under it. It also set up a system known as federalism. Under **federalism**, state and national governments share power and duties. Powers given to the states are called **reserved powers**. States, for example, have the right to create public schools. Each state also has the right to control business within its borders.

The Constitution created three branches of government. They are the legislative, executive and judicial branches. The separation of the government into three branches is called the **separation of powers**. It keeps one branch of government from becoming more powerful than others.

The writers of the constitution also included checks and balances. **Checks and balances** is a system in which each branch of government can limit the actions of the other branches. For example, the president can check the power of the Congress. He can block a law Congress passed by voting "no."

The Bill of Rights

After the Constitution was approved, it became clear that it had a flaw. It did not protect people's basic rights. Ten amendments were added to the Constitution. Each **amendment**, or change, protects our rights. The first ten amendments to the Constitution are known as the Bill of Rights.

My Social Studies Vocabulary
Go to page 94 to list other words you have learned about the Constitution.

16 The Constitution

The Constitution 17

DURING READING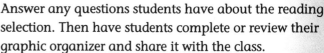

Read the selection aloud to students, as they follow along in their books, pausing at the end of each paragraph or section. Review any words or concepts that students are having trouble understanding. Remind students that there is a glossary at the back of their book that contains all of the words that appear in boldfaced type in the lesson.

- Have students pick out the three target vocabulary words that share a similar prefix (*confederation, convention, compromise*). Based on the definitions of the words, have students make an educated guess about the meaning of the prefix *con-/com-* (*together*). How do the words share the idea of "togetherness"? (*For example, in a compromise, the two sides come together when each side gives up something it wanted.*)

- Direct students' attention to the diagram on page 17. Discuss with students what each side gave up in "The Great Compromise." Point out to students that *compromise* can be used as both a noun and a verb. In this selection, *compromise* is used as a noun. Challenge students to use the word as a verb.

- Write *confederation* and *federalism* on the board. Underline the common root, *fed*. Tell students that both words come from the Latin *fides*, which means "faith." Under a federal system, the smaller political units have faith that the central government will act for the good of all.

Have students read the selection again on their own.

AFTER READING

Review Graphic Organizer

Answer any questions students have about the reading selection. Then have students complete or review their graphic organizer and share it with the class.

Summarize

Have students work together to come up with either a written or an oral summary of the lesson. Encourage students to use the target vocabulary words as the basis of their summary. Have students share their summary with the class.

My Social Studies Vocabulary

Encourage students to turn to My Social Studies Vocabulary on page 94 of the student book and use the space provided to add other words about the new nation and the Constitution.

The Constitution

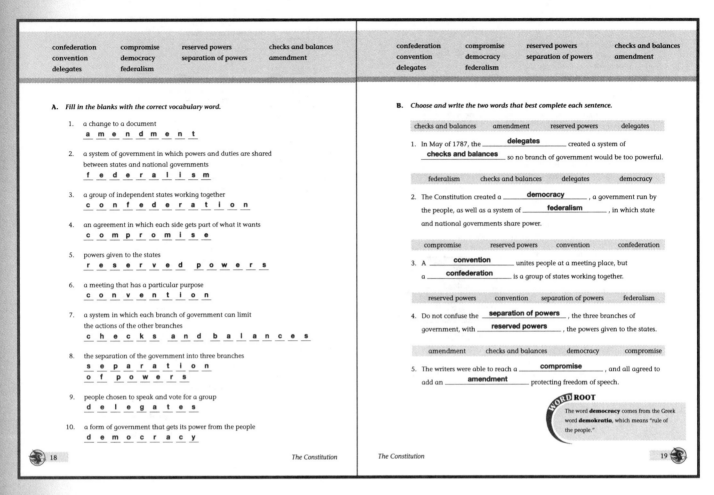

ACTIVITIES A–D

Encourage students to complete as many of the activities as possible. Remind students that they may refer to the Glossary at the back of their book as they complete the activities. Students may work independently, in small groups, or as a class. When students are done, discuss the answers for each activity.

Extensions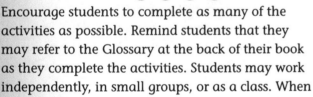

These extension ideas allow you to reuse or expand upon the activities. Share them with students who complete the activities before other students, or have students do them for additional practice with target vocabulary words.

A Do a word chop with the answers to the exercise. Draw a grid of twenty boxes. Divide each target vocabulary word in half, and write half of each word in a box somewhere on the grid. Exchange grids with a classmate, and draw arrows to the word parts that each other made.

B Put the list of target vocabulary words in alphabetical order.

WORD ROOT

Write the words *epidemic* and *democracy* on the board and have a student volunteer circle the common word part (*dem*). Tell students that an *epidemic* is an outbreak of a contagious disease that spreads rapidly among many people. Explain to students that both words have a common root *demos*, which means "people." Have students discuss how the words are related in meaning.

C Write a question for which each sentence could be the answer.

D Choose the word on the list that was the most difficult for you to define. Make up a memory device to help you remember what the word means.

confederation	compromise	reserved powers	checks and balances
convention	democracy	separation of powers	amendment
delegates	federalism		

C. *Choose the correct vocabulary word to complete each sentence.*

1. Under the system of __checks and balances__, the president can limit the power of Congress.

2. A state's __reserved powers__ include the right to create public schools.

3. Powers and duties are shared between states and the national government under the system of __federalism__.

4. Everybody gets part of what they want in a __compromise__.

5. Most people thought that their __delegates__ represented them well.

6. Three branches of government create a __separation of powers__.

7. When the Constitution needs to be changed, an __amendment__ is added.

8. The first government of the United States was a __confederation__ of states.

9. In a __democracy__, everyone has a voice in how the government is run.

10. Men from 12 states met at a __convention__ to create a new plan for governing the United States.

---

confederation	compromise	reserved powers	checks and balances
convention	democracy	separation of powers	amendment
delegates	federalism		

Students' answers will vary.

D. *Use each word in a sentence that shows you understand the meaning of the word.*

1. amendment __Adding an amendment changes our constitution.__

2. compromise __To create our constitution, people had to agree to a compromise.__

3. confederation __A confederation of states was our first government.__

4. separation of powers __If a government has only one branch, there can be no separation of powers.__

5. convention __There was a convention so people could get together and solve the country's problems.__

6. reserved powers __Powers given to states are reserved powers.__

7. democracy __In a democracy, people give their government its power.__

8. federalism __The sharing of powers between states and national governments is federalism.__

9. checks and balances __A presidential veto is part of the system of checks and balances.__

10. delegates __How many delegates from Virginia were at the convention?__

Write!
Write your response to the prompt on a separate sheet of paper. Use as many vocabulary words as you can in your writing.
What were some potential problems faced by the writers of the Constitution? How did they solve them?

Write!

Distribute Writing Graphic Organizer: Main Idea and Details Chart, Teacher Guide page 82. Suggest that students write each problem in the Main Idea box and each solution in the Details box.

Sample Answer

Delegates to the Constitutional Convention from states with many people wanted to make sure that their states had more power. Delegates from states with fewer people wanted to make sure they had equal power. The "Great Compromise," which created a Congress with two parts, solved this problem. One part of Congress has representation based on the population. In the other part, every state has equal representation.

In addition, the separation of powers among three branches of government and a system of checks and balances kept any one branch of government from becoming too strong.

TAKE-HOME ACTIVITY

Assign the Take-Home Activity to students for additional practice with the target vocabulary words. The reproducible Take-Home Activity for Lesson 3 is on page 86 of the Teacher Guide.

The Constitution

TAKE HOME 3

confederation	compromise	reserved powers	checks and balances
convention	democracy	separation of powers	amendment
delegates	federalism		

Use vocabulary words to complete the puzzle.

The Constitution

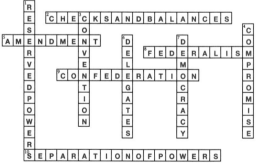

ACROSS

2 a system in which each branch of government can limit the actions of the other branches

5 a change to a document

8 a system of government in which power is shared between states and national government

9 a group of independent states working together

10 the separation of the government into three branches

DOWN

1 powers given to the states

3 a meeting that has a particular purpose

4 an agreement in which each side gets part of what it wants

6 people chosen to speak and vote for a group

7 a form of government that gets its power from the people

Tell someone in your family what you have learned about the Constitution.

LESSON 4

The Early Years of the United States

(Student Book pages 22–27)

Lesson Summary George Washington was our first president. He was the head of the executive branch of government. He had a team of advisors, or cabinet. Washington's administration had to make many decisions about the nation's economy. Many new ideas for revenue came from Alexander Hamilton. They included a tariff and an excise tax. Washington's administration also had to make a policy on the French Revolution. Washington chose neutrality.

TARGET VOCABULARY

executive branch the part of government that carries out laws

cabinet people who give advice to the president

administration a president's time in office

treasury the department in charge of collecting taxes and managing public funds

controversy a public disagreement between two sides holding opposite views

revenue the income that a government collects to pay for public expenses

tariff a tax on goods brought into the country

excise tax money paid by the maker or seller of a product

neutrality the policy of not taking sides in a war

policy a plan of action

COGNATES

Spanish-speaking students may find a discussion of the similarities and differences between English and Spanish cognates helpful.

English	Spanish
administration	administración
treasury	tesorería
controversy	controversia
tariff	tarifa
neutrality	neutralidad
policy	política

BEFORE READING

Activate Prior Knowledge

Write the term *economy* on the board. Review the term. Ask what decisions the first president and his advisors might have had to make about the economy. Record ideas. Elicit or introduce ideas about taxes. Ask what decisions the first president and his advisors might have had to make about their relationship to other countries and other countries' wars. Elicit the idea of taking or not taking sides.

Introduce Target Vocabulary

Tell students that they are about to read a selection about the early years of the United States. Write the target vocabulary words on the board. Model the pronunciation of each word and have student volunteers repeat the word. Discuss the meaning of each word and, if necessary, write the definition next to the word.

Present Graphic Organizer

Provide each student with a copy of Vocabulary Graphic Organizer: Four Square, Teacher Guide page 78. Have each student choose a target vocabulary word or assign a target word to each student. As students read, they should add information about the target vocabulary word to the graphic organizer.

> Word and Definition Cards for Lesson 4 are on pages 105 and 106 of the Teacher Guide.

VOCABULARY STRATEGY: Word Families

Remind students that they can use related words to figure out the meanings of unfamiliar words. For example, students may not know *treasury,* but they may know other words in the same word family, such as *treasure* or *treasurer.* These words can help them understand that the word *treasury* is related to money or funds. Similarly, students might know the word *neutral* and be able to identify the suffix *-ity* as a noun-making suffix that identifies *neutrality* as "the state of being neutral." Students can also learn new words once they learn a single member of a word family.

DURING READING

Read the selection aloud to students, as they follow along in their books, pausing at the end of each paragraph or section. Review any words or concepts that students are having trouble understanding. Remind students that there is a glossary at the back of their book that contains all of the words that appear in boldfaced type in the lesson.

- Ask students to imagine that your school has an executive branch. Who would be the head of it? Who might be the cabinet, or advisors?

- Note to students that the controversy between Hamilton and Jefferson was the start of our two-party political system.

- Write the word *revenue* on the board and ask students what it means. Ask students to name the two types of revenue they have just learned about. Then guide students in creating a Venn diagram that compares and contrasts a tariff and an excise tax.

- Have students give an example of a policy in your school, such as the policy related to attendance.

Talk about why policies are important. Ask students to explain why neutrality is an example of a policy.

Have students read the selection again on their own.

AFTER READING

Review Graphic Organizer

Answer any questions students have about the reading selection. Then have students complete or review their graphic organizer and share it with the class.

Summarize

Have students work together to come up with either a written or an oral summary of the lesson. Encourage students to use the target vocabulary words as the basis of their summary. Have students share their summary with the class.

My Social Studies Vocabulary

Encourage students to turn to My Social Studies Vocabulary on page 95 of the student book and use the space provided to add other words about the early years of the United States.

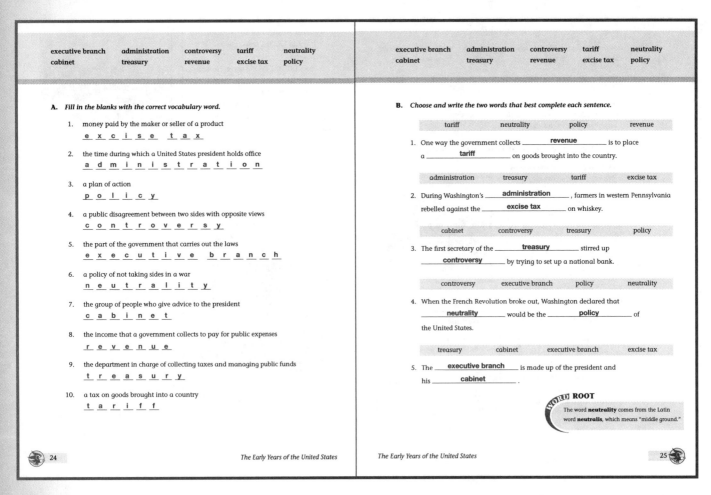

Page 24:

executive branch	administration	controversy	tariff	neutrality
cabinet	treasury	revenue	excise tax	policy

A. Fill in the blanks with the correct vocabulary word.

1. money paid by the maker or seller of a product
   e x c i s e t a x

2. the time during which a United States president holds office
   a d m i n i s t r a t i o n

3. a plan of action
   p o l i c y

4. a public disagreement between two sides with opposite views
   c o n t r o v e r s y

5. the part of the government that carries out the laws
   e x e c u t i v e b r a n c h

6. a policy of not taking sides in a war
   n e u t r a l i t y

7. the group of people who give advice to the president
   c a b i n e t

8. the income that a government collects to pay for public expenses
   r e v e n u e

9. the department in charge of collecting taxes and managing public funds
   t r e a s u r y

10. a tax on goods brought into a country
    t a r i f f

24   *The Early Years of the United States*

Page 25:

executive branch	administration	controversy	tariff	neutrality
cabinet	treasury	revenue	excise tax	policy

B. Choose and write the two words that best complete each sentence.

tariff	neutrality	policy	revenue

1. One way the government collects ___**revenue**___ is to place a ___**tariff**___ on goods brought into the country.

administration	treasury	tariff	excise tax

2. During Washington's ___**administration**___, farmers in western Pennsylvania rebelled against the ___**excise tax**___ on whiskey.

cabinet	controversy	treasury	policy

3. The first secretary of the ___**treasury**___ stirred up ___**controversy**___ by trying to set up a national bank.

controversy	executive branch	policy	neutrality

4. When the French Revolution broke out, Washington declared that ___**neutrality**___ would be the ___**policy**___ of the United States.

treasury	cabinet	executive branch	excise tax

5. The ___**executive branch**___ is made up of the president and his ___**cabinet**___.

WORD ROOT
The word **neutrality** comes from the Latin word **neutralis**, which means "middle ground."

The Early Years of the United States   25

ACTIVITIES A–D

Encourage students to complete as many of the activities as possible. Remind students that they may refer to the Glossary at the back of their book as they complete the activities. Students may work independently, in small groups, or as a class. When students are done, discuss the answers for each activity.

Extensions

These extension ideas allow you to reuse or expand upon the activities. Share them with students who complete the activities before other students, or have students do them for additional practice with target vocabulary words.

A Look up two of the target vocabulary words in the Glossary, in the dictionary, and in an encyclopedia. How are the definitions similar? How are they different?

B After you have chosen the correct answers for each sentence, explain why the wrong answers did not make sense in the sentence.

C Draw a diagram showing how any two target words are related. For example, you might use a diagram to show how one word is an example that fits in a category named by another word.

D Choose two of the target words and write a single sentence that uses them both correctly.

WORD ROOT

Note to students that other words come from this root word. List the words *neuter, neutral,* and *neutralise* on the board. Work with students to define each word. Then have students tell what the words' meaning have in common. *(All carry the meaning of being "in the middle.")*

| executive branch | administration | controversy | tariff | neutrality |
| cabinet | treasury | revenue | excise tax | policy |

C. *Choose the correct vocabulary word to complete each sentence.*

1. Hamilton's bank plan caused _____ **controversy** _____ because some people felt it would give too much power to the government.

2. The president is the head of the _____ **executive branch** _____ of government.

3. The maker of a product might need to pay an _____ **excise tax** _____ on it.

4. Washington hoped that _____ **neutrality** _____ would allow the United States to stay strong.

5. The government department that collects and manages money is the _____ **treasury** _____

6. Taxes are one source of government _____ **revenue** _____ .

7. As secretary of the treasury, Alexander Hamilton was a member of Washington's _____ **cabinet** _____ .

8. A president's _____ **administration** _____ lasts as long as his term in office.

9. By placing a _____ **tariff** _____ on imports, Hamilton hoped people would buy cheaper American goods.

10. Washington's _____ **policy** _____ of neutrality meant that the United States would not take sides in the French Revolution.

| executive branch | administration | controversy | tariff | neutrality |
| cabinet | treasury | revenue | excise tax | policy |

Students' answers will vary.

D. *Use each word in a sentence that shows you understand the meaning of the word.*

1. excise tax ___ An excise tax is a fee that a product's maker or seller pays to the government.

2. neutrality ___ When a country has a policy of neutrality, it doesn't take sides in a war.

3. administration ___ Each president's administration has different cabinet members.

4. controversy ___ When people have different ideas about government issues, there is bound to be controversy.

5. policy ___ President Washington's policy of neutrality kept the United States out of war.

6. executive branch ___ The president is the head of the executive branch of government.

7. revenue ___ A government must have revenue so it can pay its bills.

8. cabinet ___ The members of the president's cabinet give him advice.

9. tariff ___ A tariff on goods brought into the country makes them more expensive.

10. treasury ___ A government's treasury controls the government's money.

Write!

Write your response to the prompt on a separate sheet of paper. Use as many vocabulary words as you can in your writing.

Even though George Washington had no examples on which to base his presidency, he was still a strong leader. What made George Washington a strong president?

Write!

Provide each student with a copy of Writing Graphic Organizer: Main Idea and Details Chart, Teacher Guide page 82. Tell students to write the main ideas that they want to make about what made Washington a strong president in the first column. Then have them use the second column to list the details that they will use to support their main idea.

Sample Answer

   George Washington was a strong president because he knew what the country needed. He set up the first executive branch to carry out the laws. He chose good, intelligent men for his cabinet, such as Alexander Hamilton for the treasury. Even when his cabinet made decisions that caused controversy, he supported them. Washington's administration showed the country that peaceful change could be made through the Constitution. He put our country first with a policy of neutrality.

TAKE-HOME ACTIVITY

Assign the Take-Home Activity to students for additional practice with the target vocabulary words. The reproducible Take-Home Activity for Lesson 4 is on page 87 of the Teacher Guide.

The Early Years of the United States

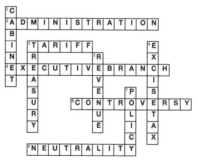

TAKE HOME 4

| executive branch | administration | controversy | tariff | neutrality |
| cabinet | treasury | revenue | excise tax | policy |

Use vocabulary words to complete the puzzle.

The Early Years of the United States

ACROSS

2 a president's time in office

3 a tax on goods brought into a country

6 the part of the government that carries out laws

8 public disagreement between two sides with opposite views

9 a policy of not taking sides during a war

DOWN

1 the group of people who give advice to the president and make up the heads of departments

3 the department in charge of collecting taxes and managing public funds

4 money paid to the government by a maker or seller of a product

5 income that a government collects to pay for public expenses

7 a plan of action

 Tell someone in your family what you have learned about the early years of the United States.

87

LESSON 5

The New Nation and the World

(Student Book pages 28–33)

Lesson Summary Great Britain and France were at war. The British tried to cut off American trade with France. The British also impressed American sailors. Soon the new nation was fighting the British in the War of 1812. One result of the war was an increase of nationalism. A few years later, a new president created a new doctrine. It said the United States would stay out of European problems. In 1828, Andrew Jackson was elected president by a landslide.

TARGET VOCABULARY

blockade to prevent ships from entering or leaving a port

impress to force a person into military service

embargo a ban on exporting goods

armistice an agreement to stop fighting

territory land under the control of a country

nationalism pride in one's country

doctrine a statement of government policy

landslide the winning of an election by a very large majority of votes

spoils system the practice of giving jobs to supporters

veto to say or vote "no"

COGNATES

Spanish-speaking students may find a discussion of the similarities and differences between English and Spanish cognates helpful.

English	Spanish
blockade	bloquear
embargo	embargo
territory	territorio
nationalism	nacionalismo
doctrine	doctrina
veto	vetar

BEFORE READING

Activate Prior Knowledge

Write these two headings in a two-column chart on the board: "Words Related to War" and "Words Related to Presidents." Invite students to place any target vocabulary words they know, or think that they might know, in a category and to give a reason why. Record their answers. After students complete the reading and activities in this lesson, return to the chart. Discuss possible changes, as well as words that might fit in both categories.

Introduce Target Vocabulary

Tell students that they are about to read a selection about the new nation and the world. Write the target vocabulary words on the board. Model the pronunciation of each word and have student volunteers repeat the word. Discuss the meaning of each word and, if necessary, write the definition next to the word.

Present Graphic Organizer

Provide each student with a copy of Vocabulary Graphic Organizer: Vocabulary Circle, Teacher Guide page 79. Have students choose a target vocabulary word or assign one to them, and have them write it in the center of the circle. As they read, students should add information about the target vocabulary word to the outer spaces of the circle.

> Word and Definition Cards for Lesson 5 are on pages 107 and 108 of the Teacher Guide.

VOCABULARY STRATEGY: Context Clues

Remind students to use context clues to find the meanings of unfamiliar words. Explain that some context clues are synonyms or other statements of a word's meaning. Have students find the word *embargo* on page 28. Point out how the definition for *embargo* begins with the word *or*. Explain that from the context, students can figure out that an *embargo* keeps goods from leaving a country.

The New Nation and the World

LESSON 5

blockade embargo territory doctrine spoils system
impress armistice nationalism landslide veto

The presidents who followed Washington worked on building the nation. But they could not avoid dealing with the rest of the world. Read this selection to find out why.

The New Nation and the World

British Threats to American Shipping

Great Britain was opposed to the French Revolution and became France's enemy. Great Britain tried to **blockade** France. But the British could only partly prevent ships from entering or leaving French ports. Then the British began to seize American ships. The British needed more sailors. They claimed that American sailors were British and impressed them into the British navy. To **impress** is to force a person into military service. But the thousands of impressed sailors were not British.

In 1807, President Thomas Jefferson tried to solve the problem. He ordered an **embargo**, or ban, on goods leaving America. That kept American ships at home. Jefferson hoped this action would force Great Britain and France to honor American neutrality. Instead, it hurt American trade.

American sailors were impressed because the British needed people to work on their ships.

The War of 1812

In 1812, President James Madison decided to go to war. He thought that the United States could gain Canada in the war against Great Britain. But the British won most of the early battles. They even captured Washington, D.C.

At last, Great Britain and the United States declared an **armistice**. It put an end to the fighting. Neither country gained any territory. **Territory** is land under the control of a country. But the United States showed that it could stand up to the world's strongest power. The war led to a rise of **nationalism**, meaning that Americans had more pride in their country.

When James Monroe became president, he worked on keeping the nation strong. In 1823, he presented a doctrine. A **doctrine** is a statement of government policy. The Monroe Doctrine warned Europe not to set up new colonies in the Americas. It promised that the United States would stay out of Europe's affairs.

The Monroe Doctrine set policy for the Americas.

The Age of Jackson

Andrew Jackson won the 1828 election by a **landslide**. He received a large majority of votes. After Jackson took office, he fired many government workers. He gave their jobs to people who helped him get elected. The practice of giving jobs to supporters is called the **spoils system**.

President Jackson did not approve of the Bank of the United States. He thought it had too much power over state banks. When it came time to renew the bank's contract, Jackson vetoed it. To **veto** means to say or vote "no."

Andrew Jackson was a general and a hero of the War of 1812.

My Social Studies Vocabulary
Go to page 95 to list other words you have learned about the new nation and the world.

28   The New Nation and the World

The New Nation and the World   29

DURING READING 👂 👄 📖

Read the selection aloud to students, as they follow along in their books, pausing at the end of each paragraph or section. Review any words or concepts that students are having trouble understanding. Remind students that there is a glossary at the back of their book that contains all of the words that appear in boldfaced type in the lesson.

- Draw a sketch representing the United States, Europe, the ocean, and a blockade near the coast of the United States. Ask students to identify the part of the sketch that shows the blockade.

- Work with students to complete a *who, what, when, where,* and *why* organizer for the term *embargo*.

- Ask students which target vocabulary word is a closed compound; one word made up of two smaller words (*landslide*). Point out to students that *landslide* has more than one meaning. Ask students what the other meaning is (*the rapid movement of dirt and rocks down the side of a hill or mountain*). Have students explain how the two meanings are connected.

- Point out to students that *spoils system* is also a compound word. Have students define each word in the compound.

Have students read the selection again on their own.

AFTER READING

Review Graphic Organizer 👂 👄 ✏️
Answer any questions students have about the reading selection. Then have students complete or review their graphic organizer and share it with the class.

Summarize 👄 👂 ✏️
Have students work together to come up with either a written or an oral summary of the lesson. Encourage students to use the target vocabulary words as the basis of their summary. Have students share their summary with the class.

My Social Studies Vocabulary 📖 ✏️
Encourage students to turn to My Social Studies Vocabulary on page 95 of the student book and use the space provided to add other words about the new nation and the world.

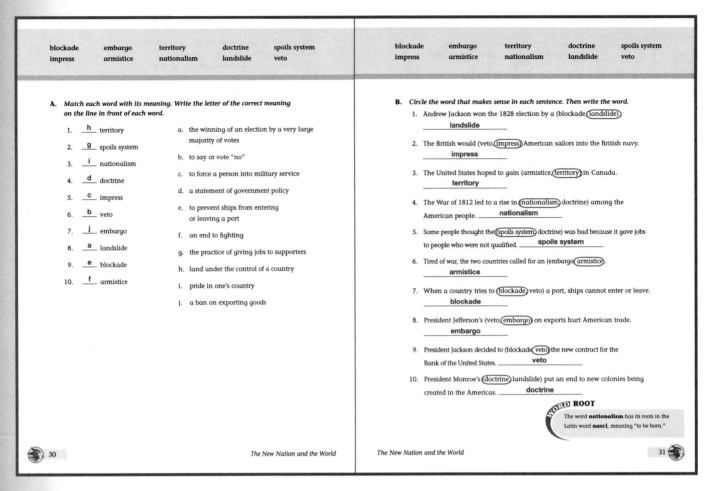

| blockade | embargo | territory | doctrine | spoils system |
| impress | armistice | nationalism | landslide | veto |

A. Match each word with its meaning. Write the letter of the correct meaning on the line in front of each word.

1. __h__ territory
2. __g__ spoils system
3. __i__ nationalism
4. __d__ doctrine
5. __c__ impress
6. __b__ veto
7. __j__ embargo
8. __a__ landslide
9. __e__ blockade
10. __f__ armistice

a. the winning of an election by a very large majority of votes
b. to say or vote "no"
c. to force a person into military service
d. a statement of government policy
e. to prevent ships from entering or leaving a port
f. an end to fighting
g. the practice of giving jobs to supporters
h. land under the control of a country
i. pride in one's country
j. a ban on exporting goods

B. Circle the word that makes sense in each sentence. Then write the word.

1. Andrew Jackson won the 1828 election by a (blockade, landslide). __landslide__
2. The British would (veto, impress) American sailors into the British navy. __impress__
3. The United States hoped to gain (armistice, territory) in Canada. __territory__
4. The War of 1812 led to a rise in (nationalism, doctrine) among the American people. __nationalism__
5. Some people thought the (spoils system, doctrine) was bad because it gave jobs to people who were not qualified. __spoils system__
6. Tired of war, the two countries called for an (embargo, armistice). __armistice__
7. When a country tries to (blockade, veto) a port, ships cannot enter or leave. __blockade__
8. President Jefferson's (veto, embargo) on exports hurt American trade. __embargo__
9. President Jackson decided to (blockade, veto) the new contract for the Bank of the United States. __veto__
10. President Monroe's (doctrine, landslide) put an end to new colonies being created in the Americas. __doctrine__

ROOT
The word **nationalism** has its roots in the Latin word **nasci**, meaning "to be born."

30 · The New Nation and the World

The New Nation and the World · 31

ACTIVITIES A–D

Encourage students to complete as many of the activities as possible. Remind students that they may refer to the Glossary at the back of their book as they complete the activities. Students may work independently, in small groups, or as a class. When students are done, discuss the answers for each activity.

Extensions

These extension ideas allow you to reuse or expand upon the activities. Share them with students who complete the activities before other students, or have students do them for additional practice with target vocabulary words.

A Put the target vocabulary words in alphabetical order.

B Rewrite each sentence as a question.

C Make a two-column chart with these headings: "Nouns (Naming Words)" and "Verbs (Action Words)." Sort the words into the correct column according to how they are used on pages 28–29.

WORD ROOT

Tell students that other words that share the same root with *nationalism* are *nationality* and *nature*. Have students relate these words to the meaning of "to be born."

D Choose one of the target vocabulary words and use it to create a poem or rap about the lesson. Write the word vertically down a sheet of paper, one letter per line. Have that letter serve as the first letter of the first word of that line of the poem.

C. *Choose the correct vocabulary word to complete each sentence.*

1. The war ended when the nations called for an _____armistice_____ .

2. The president has the right to _____veto_____ any law.

3. President Jefferson wanted an _____embargo_____ to force Great Britain and France to accept the neutrality of the United States.

4. On the Fourth of July, people show their _____nationalism_____ by waving flags.

5. Because the British needed sailors, they might _____impress_____ an American sailor into the British navy.

6. Jackson was the first president to use the _____spoils system_____ to fill government jobs.

7. After the War of 1812, Great Britain kept its _____territory_____ in Canada.

8. Great Britain's attempt to _____blockade_____ French ports was only partly successful.

9. President Monroe set forth a _____doctrine_____ to prevent European countries from gaining more control in the Americas.

10. Someone who wins an election by a _____landslide_____ wins a very large majority of the votes.

Students' answers will vary.

D. *Use each pair of words in a sentence.*

1. blockade, territory
   Great Britain tried to blockade French ports and gain territory in the United States.

2. embargo, impress
   President Jefferson did not want the British to impress American sailors, so he put an embargo on American goods.

3. doctrine, nationalism
   A doctrine that makes a country strong will probably stir people's feelings of nationalism.

4. landslide, spoils system
   Because President Jackson won the election by a landslide, he might not have worried about objections to a spoils system.

5. veto, armistice
   The war continued when one country said they would veto any armistice.

Write!
Write your response to the prompt on a separate sheet of paper. Use as many vocabulary words as you can in your writing.

Explain the steps that the United States took to deal with other countries during the early 1800s.

Write!

Provide each student with a copy of Writing Graphic Organizer: Sequence Chart, Teacher Guide page 81. Tell students to use one box to write in order each step that the United States took. If they need more space, they can draw more boxes on the back of their paper.

Sample Answer

In the early 1800s, Great Britain blockaded France. The United States tried to keep out of the conflict, but British ships captured American ships and impressed American sailors. So, in 1807, the president ordered an embargo, but that only hurt American business because they needed to sell and buy foreign goods. Since neutrality didn't work, President Madison decided to enter the war against Great Britain. He also hoped to add Canada as an American territory. The war ended, however, with no gains.

TAKE-HOME ACTIVITY

Assign the Take-Home Activity to students for additional practice with the target vocabulary words. The reproducible Take-Home Activity for Lesson 5 is on page 88 of the Teacher Guide.

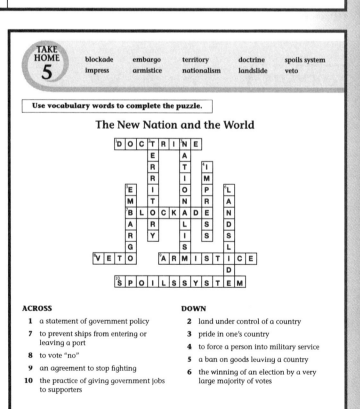

TAKE HOME 5

| blockade | embargo | territory | doctrine | spoils system |
| impress | armistice | nationalism | landslide | veto |

Use vocabulary words to complete the puzzle.

The New Nation and the World

ACROSS
1 a statement of government policy
7 to prevent ships from entering or leaving a port
8 to vote "no"
9 an agreement to stop fighting
10 the practice of giving government jobs to supporters

DOWN
2 land under control of a country
3 pride in one's country
4 to force a person into military service
5 a ban on goods leaving a country
6 the winning of an election by a very large majority of votes

Tell someone in your family what you have learned about the new nation and the world.

88   ©Curriculum Associates, Inc. *Passwords: Social Studies Vocabulary, United States History: The Constitution to 1920, Lesson 5*

The New Nation and the World

LESSON 6

Settling the West

(Student Book pages 34–39)

TARGET VOCABULARY

opportunity a chance to make money or to better oneself

pioneer one of the first people to settle an area

adjoining connected or next to other things

frontier an area with few people on the edge of a settled region

turnpike a road that travelers pay to use

technology the use of scientific knowledge to make new machines and tools

canal a waterway that connects two bodies of water

freight goods carried by truck, train, ship, or airplane

ordinance a rule or law passed by a government

homeland the land that a person comes from

COGNATES

Spanish-speaking students may find a discussion of the similarities and differences between English and Spanish cognates helpful.

English	Spanish
opportunity	oportunidad
pioneer	pionero
frontier	frontera
technology	tecnología
canal	canal
ordinance	ordenanza

Lesson Summary Americans continued to look west. Pioneers saw the opportunity for cheap land and a new life. Travel was hard. New technology, however, began to change travel. The steamboat led to more river travel. Canals and a new kind of road, the turnpike, made it easier and cheaper to move people and freight. The Northwest Ordinance stated that a territory having 60,000 people could apply to be a state. The government moved Native Americans from their homeland to make way for the settlers.

BEFORE READING

Activate Prior Knowledge

Have students fill out a KWL chart about the settling the West. Tell them to write two things in the first column that they already know about why people went west, how people went west, or the improvements that made going west possible. In the second column, have students write two questions that they have about settling the West. Once students have completed the chart, have the class share what they know and want to learn. Return to the charts when students have completed the lesson so that they can fill out the last column with things they have learned.

Introduce Target Vocabulary

Tell students that they are about to read a selection about settling the West. Write the target vocabulary words on the board. Model the pronunciation of each word and have student volunteers repeat the word. Discuss the meaning of each word and, if necessary, write the definition next to the word.

Present Graphic Organizer

Provide each student with a copy of Vocabulary Graphic Organizer: Vocabulary Map, Teacher Guide page 77. Have students choose or assign each student a target vocabulary word. As they read, students should complete as many parts of the Vocabulary Map as they can.

> Word and Definition Cards for Lesson 6 are on pages 109 and 110 of the Teacher Guide.

VOCABULARY STRATEGY: Using Illustrations and Photographs

Remind students that illustrations and photographs, especially in textbooks, can help them understand unfamiliar words by providing a visual explanation or example of them. Point out how the illustrations on pages 34–35 provide meaning and context for some of the target vocabulary words. Encourage students to refer to the illustrations, here and in their other reading, to expand their knowledge of unfamiliar words and to get a better sense of the context as a whole.

Settling the West

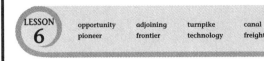

LESSON 6

| opportunity | adjoining | turnpike | canal | ordinance |
| pioneer | frontier | technology | freight | homeland |

After the American Revolution, people began moving west of the Appalachian Mountains. Read this selection to find out how that movement enlarged the United States and brought more states into the union.

Settling the West

The Country Grows

People in the thirteen states were searching for cheaper land. They were also looking for better opportunities. An **opportunity** is a chance to make money or to better oneself. So, pioneers began moving to open land out West. A **pioneer** is one of the first people to settle an area.

Between 1800 and 1810, the population of Ohio increased from 45,000 to more than 230,000. The number of people in Kentucky, Tennessee, and the lands **adjoining**, or next to, them also grew.

In 1803, France sold the Louisiana Territory, which it had gained from Spain, to the United States. This new frontier doubled the size of the United States. A **frontier** is an area with few people at the edge of a settled region.

The Louisiana Territory doubled the size of the United States.

Improvements in Transportation

Travel to the West was not easy. Roads were rough, narrow trails. Soon private companies started building turnpikes. A **turnpike** is a road that travelers have to pay to use. Then the government built the National Road. It stretched from Maryland to Illinois.

Technology is the use of scientific knowledge to make machines and tools. It helped travel. The steamboat made river trips faster.

Robert Fulton's Clermont was the first successful steamboat. In 1807, it made its first trip up the Hudson River.

Not all bodies of water were connected. So, canals were dug. A **canal** is a waterway that connects two bodies of water. The Erie Canal was the first major canal in the United States. It greatly reduced the cost of moving people and freight. **Freight** is goods carried by a ship, truck, train, or airplane.

Settlers Go West

In 1787, Congress passed an **ordinance** so that lands north and west of the Ohio River could become states. This rule, or law, was called the Northwest Ordinance. It stated that a territory could apply to be a state once it had 60,000 people.

Native Americans fought back. They did not want white settlers on their land. In 1830, Congress passed the Indian Removal Act. Native Americans would be forced from their **homeland**, or land they came from. They would be resettled west of the Mississippi River.

So many Cherokee died on the trip from their homeland, they called it the "Trail of Tears."

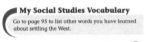
My Social Studies Vocabulary
Go to page 95 to list other words you have learned about settling the West.

34   Settling the West

Settling the West   35

DURING READING

Read the selection aloud to students, as they follow along in their books, pausing at the end of each paragraph or section. Review any words or concepts that students are having trouble understanding. Remind students that there is a glossary at the back of their book that contains all of the words that appear in boldfaced type in the lesson.

- Ask students to give examples of an opportunity they have or an opportunity someone else has whom they know.

- Draw a Venn diagram to compare and contrast the terms *turnpike* and *canal*. Guide students to complete it.

- Remind students that a compound word is a word made by putting two smaller words together. Ask students what two small words were joined to create the word *homeland*. Discuss with students how thinking about the two small words that make up the larger compound word will help them remember the meaning of the word.

Have students read the selection again on their own.

AFTER READING

Review Graphic Organizer

Answer any questions students have about the reading selection. Then have students complete or review their graphic organizer and share it with the class.

Summarize

Have students work together to come up with either a written or an oral summary of the lesson. Encourage students to use the target vocabulary words as the basis of their summary. Have students share their summary with the class.

My Social Studies Vocabulary

Encourage students to turn to My Social Studies Vocabulary on page 95 of the student book and use the space provided to add other words about settling the West.

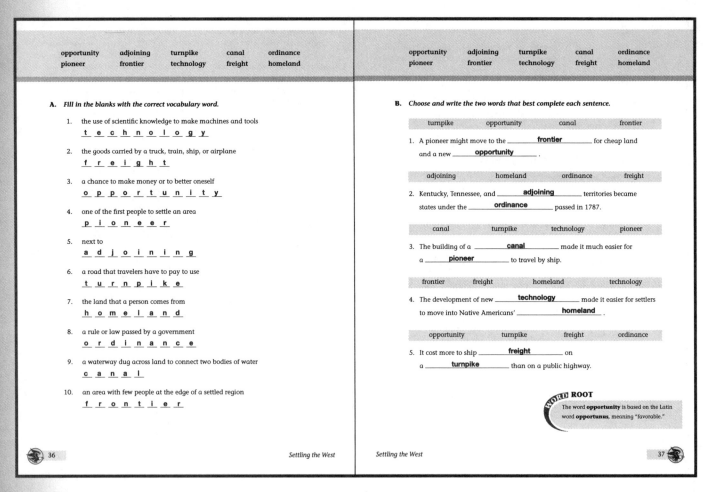

A. Fill in the blanks with the correct vocabulary word.

1. the use of scientific knowledge to make machines and tools
   t e c h n o l o g y

2. the goods carried by a truck, train, ship, or airplane
   f r e i g h t

3. a chance to make money or to better oneself
   o p p o r t u n i t y

4. one of the first people to settle an area
   p i o n e e r

5. next to
   a d j o i n i n g

6. a road that travelers have to pay to use
   t u r n p i k e

7. the land that a person comes from
   h o m e l a n d

8. a rule or law passed by a government
   o r d i n a n c e

9. a waterway dug across land to connect two bodies of water
   c a n a l

10. an area with few people at the edge of a settled region
    f r o n t i e r

B. Choose and write the two words that best complete each sentence.

| turnpike | opportunity | canal | frontier |

1. A pioneer might move to the **frontier** for cheap land and a new **opportunity**.

| adjoining | homeland | ordinance | freight |

2. Kentucky, Tennessee, and **adjoining** territories became states under the **ordinance** passed in 1787.

| canal | turnpike | technology | pioneer |

3. The building of a **canal** made it much easier for a **pioneer** to travel by ship.

| frontier | freight | homeland | technology |

4. The development of new **technology** made it easier for settlers to move into Native Americans' **homeland**.

| opportunity | turnpike | freight | ordinance |

5. It cost more to ship **freight** on a **turnpike** than on a public highway.

ROOT
The word **opportunity** is based on the Latin word **opportunus**, meaning "favorable."

ACTIVITIES A–D

Encourage students to complete as many of the activities as possible. Remind students that they may refer to the Glossary at the back of their book as they complete the activities. Students may work independently, in small groups, or as a class. When students are done, discuss the answers for each activity.

Extensions

These extension ideas allow you to reuse or expand upon the activities. Share them with students who complete the activities before other students, or have students do them for additional practice with target vocabulary words.

A Put the target vocabulary words in alphabetical order.

B Do a word chop with the answers to the exercise. Draw a grid of 20 boxes. Divide each target word in half, and write half of each word in a box somewhere in the grid. Exchange grids with a partner, and draw arrows to the word parts that each other made.

C Many of the target vocabulary words contain smaller words. For example, *technology* includes *no, long, ten,* and *lone.* Make a list of all the smaller words you can find in the one target vocabulary word.

D Draw a picture or diagram to illustrate two of the target vocabulary words.

WORD ROOT

Remind students of the meaning of the suffix *-ist* (*one who is or does*). Write the word *opportunist* on the board. Discuss the meaning of the word with students (*a person who uses opportunities to his or her advantage*). Point out to students that *opportunist* often is used negatively. Discuss why this is.

C. *Choose the correct vocabulary word to complete each sentence.*

1. Native Americans did not want to move away from their _____ **homeland** _____ .

2. Technology made it possible to travel by steamboat on a _____ **canal** _____ that connected two rivers.

3. The cost of carrying _____ **freight** _____ , such as farm goods, was much higher by land than by canal.

4. Pioneers paid a fee to go on a _____ **turnpike** _____ , but the road was much easier to travel.

5. Once the United States purchased the Louisiana Territory, many pioneers moved to the new _____ **frontier** _____ .

6. People moved west because it was an _____ **opportunity** _____ to get land.

7. The steamboat is an example of _____ **technology** _____ that made travel faster and easier.

8. People moved to states _____ **adjoining** _____ unsettled land.

9. Congress passed an _____ **ordinance** _____ in 1787 so that territories north and west of the Ohio River could become states.

10. Until turnpikes and the first highway were built, a _____ **pioneer** _____ had to travel on rough, narrow trails.

Students' answers will vary.

D. *Use each word in a sentence that shows you understand the meaning of the word.*

1. frontier **The American frontier kept moving west as people settled new areas.**

2. turnpike **Travel on a turnpike was expensive but comfortable.**

3. ordinance **When an ordinance is passed, it becomes a law.**

4. opportunity **Early settlers wanted the opportunity to own land.**

5. freight **It can be expensive to ship freight long distances.**

6. canal **A canal allowed goods and people to travel by boat instead of overland.**

7. homeland **Settlers wanted to farm on Native Americans' homeland.**

8. technology **Steamboats were one use of technology.**

9. pioneer **A pioneer left behind the comfort and safety of civilization.**

10. adjoining **States adjoining the Louisiana Territory grew rapidly.**

Write!

Write your response to the prompt on a separate sheet of paper. Use as many vocabulary words as you can in your writing.

Imagine that you own a company that wants to build a road or a canal. Write a letter to the government explaining why the road or canal should be built.

Write!

Provide each student with a copy of Writing Graphic Organizer: Topic Web, Teacher Guide page 80. Tell students to write their main idea about a road or canal in the top circle. Then have them use the other circles to list reasons or other support for their writing aim or goal.

Sample Answer

With countless pioneers ready to travel to the western frontier, what this country really needs is more roads. We at Roads, Inc. have the technology needed to cross the Appalachians and reach all the states and their adjoining territories. Our road can carry more people and more freight than the National Road. We foresee a turnpike, on which the government would collect the tolls once the road is paid for. We would like the opportunity to explain our plan in greater detail.

TAKE-HOME ACTIVITY

Assign the Take-Home Activity to students for additional practice with the target vocabulary words. The reproducible Take-Home Activity for Lesson 6 is on page 89 of the Teacher Guide.

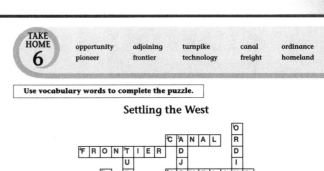

TAKE HOME 6

| opportunity | adjoining | turnpike | canal | ordinance |
| pioneer | frontier | technology | freight | homeland |

Use vocabulary words to complete the puzzle.

Settling the West

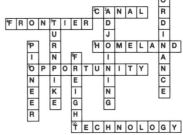

ACROSS

2 a waterway that connects two bodies of water

4 an area of few people at the edge of a settled area

7 the land that a person comes from

9 a chance to make money or to better oneself

10 the use of scientific knowledge to make machines and tools

DOWN

1 a rule or law

3 next to

5 a road that travelers have to pay to use

6 one of the first people to settle an area

8 goods carried by a ship, truck, train, or airplane

 Tell someone in your family what you have learned about settling the West.

LESSON 7
An Expanding Nation

(Student Book pages 40–45)

Lesson Summary During the 1840s, people in the United States believed that the nation had a manifest destiny to spread from coast to coast. Expansion included gaining lands in Oregon Country. It included the decision to annex Texas. The United States also gained lands that include California and other areas through war with Mexico. Capitalism produced great economic growth. Entrepreneurs were eager to do business in new places.

TARGET VOCABULARY

boundary a border

Manifest Destiny a belief that the United States should expand from the Atlantic to the Pacific Ocean

expansion an increase in size

latitude the distance north or south of the equator

land grant public land given by a government

annex to add to something larger

mass production the process of making large quantities of things by machine

economy all the business dealings of a country or state

capitalism a system in which private businesses control production

entrepreneur someone who starts a business

COGNATES

Spanish-speaking students may find a discussion of the similarities and differences between English and Spanish cognates helpful.

English	Spanish
expansion	expansión
latitude	latitud
annex	anexar
capitalism	capitalismo

BEFORE READING

Activate Prior Knowledge

Write each target vocabulary word on the board and have students rate their knowledge of it on a scale. For example, write *expansion*, have students copy the word, and then have them decide and write whether they know it, think they have some idea of what it means, or do not know it all. Return to this list again after reading to discuss how their knowledge of each word has changed.

Introduce Target Vocabulary

Tell students that they are about to read a selection about an expanding nation. Model the pronunciation of each target vocabulary word and have student volunteers repeat the word. Discuss the meaning of each word and, if necessary, write the definition next to the word.

Present Graphic Organizer

Provide each student with a copy of Vocabulary Graphic Organizer: Word Chart, Teacher Guide page 76. Have students choose or assign each student a target vocabulary word. As they read, students should complete the graphic organizer.

> Word and Definition Cards
> for Lesson 7 are on pages 111 and 112
> of the Teacher Guide.

VOCABULARY STRATEGY: Context Clues

Review the context clue signal words students have already learned for finding definitions: *is, are, means,* and *or.* Explain that some context clues are signaled by punctuation. Sometimes, a word's definition is enclosed in commas. Have students find *expansion* in the text on page 40 and circle the comma that immediately follows it. Then have them find the next comma and circle it. Note that the commas enclose the meaning of *expansion.*

LESSON 7

boundary	expansion	land grant	mass production	capitalism
Manifest Destiny	latitude	annex	economy	entrepreneur

Americans believed it was their mission to extend the borders of the United States "from sea to shining sea." How do you think the nation was able to expand from coast to coast? Read this selection to find out.

An Expanding Nation

Adding Territory

During the 1840s, Americans believed that the United States had the right to spread its rule. It was clear to them that the country should extend its boundaries from the Atlantic Ocean to the Pacific Ocean. A **boundary** is a border. A newspaper writer made up a phrase for this new belief. He called it **Manifest Destiny**.

Oregon Country

The nation's **expansion**, or increase in size, involved taking land claimed by other countries. Oregon Country was a huge area in the Northwest. The United States and Great Britain had jointly owned the land. In 1846, they agreed to divide it. The dividing line was 49 degrees north latitude. **Latitude** is the distance north or south of the equator. The equator is an imaginary line around the middle of Earth. Great Britain got the land above 49 degrees north latitude. The United States got the land below it. That land later became Oregon, Washington, and Idaho.

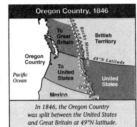

Oregon Country, 1846

In 1846, the Oregon Country was split between the United States and Great Britain at 49°N latitude.

Texas

Texas was once part of Mexico. Mexico itself was part of Spain. In 1821, Mexico broke free from Spain. It then offered Americans land grants to settle in Texas. A **land grant** is public land given by a government. The Texas settlers grew unhappy with the Mexican government. In 1836, they fought for independence and won. Texas asked to be annexed to the United States. To **annex** means to add to something larger or more important. In 1845, Texas became a state.

California and Other Western Territories

California and New Mexico were once part of Mexico, too. The United States wanted to buy those lands, but Mexico refused to sell. The United States went to war and defeated Mexico. In 1848, Mexico had to give much of its territory to the United States. This land now forms the states of California, Arizona, Nevada, and Utah. It also makes up parts of New Mexico, Colorado, and Wyoming.

After the Mexican-American War, California was admitted as a state.

Adding Markets

The need for new markets was one reason that expansion was important. Goods could be sold more cheaply due to **mass production**. This is the process of making things in large amounts, usually by machine. An **economy** is all the business dealings of a country or state. In the United States, the economy is based on **capitalism**. In this system, privately owned businesses control the production of goods. Under capitalism, entrepreneurs are always looking for new markets. An **entrepreneur** is someone who starts a business. That person takes all the risks but gets all the profits.

My Social Studies Vocabulary
Go to page 96 to list other words you have learned about the expanding nation.

DURING READING

Read the selection aloud to students, as they follow along in their books, pausing at the end of each paragraph or section. Review any words or concepts that students are having trouble understanding. Remind students that there is a glossary at the back of their book that contains all of the words that appear in boldfaced type in the lesson.

- Ask for an example of recent expansion in your school, town, or city. For instance, students might name a recent addition to your school, library, or community safety facility. Ask students what an expansion of a nation would include. Elicit or introduce the term *annex*.

- Have students identify two or more lines of latitude on a globe. Note how one line is north or south of the other line.

- Write the term *capitalism*. Ask students which two target words are most closely related to it and why (*mass production* and *entrepreneur*). Ask why mass production means more profits. Discuss why an entrepreneur would be in favor of gaining new lands in which to do business.

Have students read the selection again on their own.

AFTER READING

Review Graphic Organizer

Answer any questions students have about the reading selection. Then have students complete or review their graphic organizer and share it with the class.

Summarize

Have students work together to come up with either a written or an oral summary of the lesson. Encourage students to use the target vocabulary words as the basis of their summary. Have students share their summary with the class.

My Social Studies Vocabulary

Encourage students to turn to My Social Studies Vocabulary on page 96 of the student book and use the space provided to add other words about an expanding nation.

An Expanding Nation   41

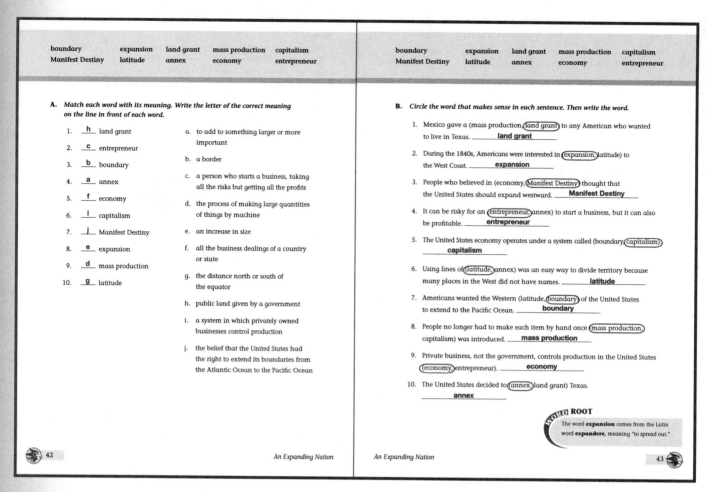

boundary   expansion   land grant   mass production   capitalism
Manifest Destiny   latitude   annex   economy   entrepreneur

A. *Match each word with its meaning. Write the letter of the correct meaning on the line in front of each word.*

1. __h__ land grant
2. __c__ entrepreneur
3. __b__ boundary
4. __a__ annex
5. __f__ economy
6. __i__ capitalism
7. __j__ Manifest Destiny
8. __e__ expansion
9. __d__ mass production
10. __g__ latitude

a. to add to something larger or more important

b. a border

c. a person who starts a business, taking all the risks but getting all the profits

d. the process of making large quantities of things by machine

e. an increase in size

f. all the business dealings of a country or state

g. the distance north or south of the equator

h. public land given by a government

i. a system in which privately owned businesses control production

j. the belief that the United States had the right to extend its boundaries from the Atlantic Ocean to the Pacific Ocean

---

boundary   expansion   land grant   mass production   capitalism
Manifest Destiny   latitude   annex   economy   entrepreneur

B. *Circle the word that makes sense in each sentence. Then write the word.*

1. Mexico gave a (mass production, land grant) to any American who wanted to live in Texas. _____land grant_____

2. During the 1840s, Americans were interested in (expansion, latitude) to the West Coast. _____expansion_____

3. People who believed in (economy, Manifest Destiny) thought that the United States should expand westward. _____Manifest Destiny_____

4. It can be risky for an (entrepreneur, annex) to start a business, but it can also be profitable. _____entrepreneur_____

5. The United States economy operates under a system called (boundary, capitalism) _____capitalism_____

6. Using lines of (latitude, annex) was an easy way to divide territory because many places in the West did not have names. _____latitude_____

7. Americans wanted the Western (latitude, boundary) of the United States to extend to the Pacific Ocean. _____boundary_____

8. People no longer had to make each item by hand once (mass production, capitalism) was introduced. _____mass production_____

9. Private business, not the government, controls production in the United States (economy, entrepreneur). _____economy_____

10. The United States decided to (annex, land grant) Texas. _____annex_____

WORD ROOT
The word **expansion** comes from the Latin word **expandere**, meaning "to spread out."

An Expanding Nation 42

An Expanding Nation 43

ACTIVITIES A–D

Encourage students to complete as many of the activities as possible. Remind students that they may refer to the Glossary at the back of their book as they complete the activities. Students may work independently, in small groups, or as a class. When students are done, discuss the answers for each activity.

Extensions

These extension ideas allow you to reuse or expand upon the activities. Share them with students who complete the activities before other students, or have students do them for additional practice with target vocabulary words.

A Choose one of the vocabulary words and make a diagram, picture, or cartoon to show its meaning.

B Choose four target words and scramble the letters. Exchange papers with a partner and unscramble each other's words.

WORD ROOT

Write the word *expansion* on the board and have a student volunteer circle the prefix and tell its meaning (*ex-* means "out"). Ask students for other words that begin with *ex-* that have the meaning "out." Students may mention *exhale, exit, exhaust, except,* or *expel.*

C Write five target vocabulary words that have a word part (prefix, suffix, root word, or base word) that is familiar to you. Underline the word part. Next to the word target word, write another word you know with the same word part.

D Circle the nouns and underline the verbs in each sentence you wrote.

An Expanding Nation

C. *Choose the correct vocabulary word to complete each sentence.*

1. The United States decided to _____**annex**_____ Texas, which became a state in 1845.

2. More goods were produced through _____**mass production**_____ .

3. The United States has an _____**economy**_____ in which private businesses control how goods are made.

4. In the United States, the growth of the economy depends on a system called _____**capitalism**_____ .

5. If someone is willing to take a risk and spend money on a new business, that person is an _____**entrepreneur**_____ .

6. The British kept the land in Oregon Country that was above 49 degrees north _____**latitude**_____ .

7. The phrase used to describe the belief that the United States should extend its rule is _____**Manifest Destiny**_____ .

8. The need for new markets was one reason for the _____**expansion**_____ of the nation.

9. In exchange for receiving a _____**land grant**_____ from Mexico, an American agreed to become a Mexican citizen.

10. The Atlantic Ocean served as the _____**boundary**_____ of the country on the East Coast.

Students' answers will vary.

D. *Use each word in a sentence that shows you understand the meaning of the word.*

1. expansion **America's expansion happened rather quickly.**

2. latitude **A line of latitude runs east and west around Earth.**

3. entrepreneur **An entrepreneur took many risks in starting a business.**

4. land grant **Americans agreed to become Mexican citizens in exchange for a land grant in Mexico.**

5. annex **The United States agreed to annex Texas.**

6. Manifest Destiny **Americans' belief that the United States should stretch from coast to coast was called Manifest Destiny.**

7. capitalism **Capitalism has given the United States a strong economy.**

8. boundary **The western boundary of the United States is the Pacific Ocean.**

9. mass production **Mass production created many items that were alike.**

10. economy **A government decides what kind of economy is best for the country.**

Write!

Write your response to the prompt on a separate sheet of paper. Use as many vocabulary words as you can in your writing.

Explain the factors that led the United States to expand during the 1840s. Give examples of America's growth.

Write!

Provide each student with a copy of Writing Graphic Organizer: Main Idea and Details Chart page 82. Suggest that students work in pairs to write two main reasons why the United States expanded in the left column. Then have them use the right column to list details that support each main reason. Ask students to use the organizer to write their own responses.

Sample Answer

There are two reasons for the United States' expansion during the 1840s. First, people believed that it was America's Manifest Destiny to stretch from coast to coast. During this time, western areas were annexed either peacefully or as a result of war. Second, business people wanted new markets for their goods. Mass production created more goods. Capitalism encouraged entrepreneurs to take advantage of the situation. Thus, the country expanded and the economy grew.

TAKE-HOME ACTIVITY

Assign the Take-Home Activity to students for additional practice with the target vocabulary words. The reproducible Take-Home Activity for Lesson 7 is on page 90 of the Teacher Guide.

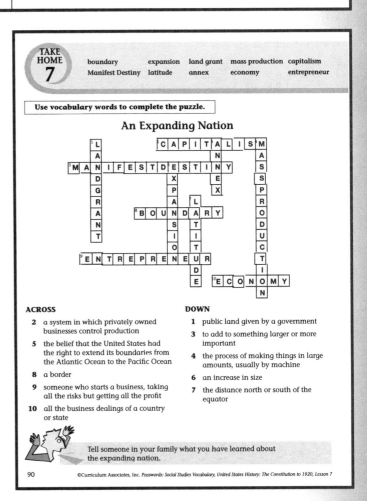

TAKE HOME 7

Use vocabulary words to complete the puzzle.

An Expanding Nation

Crossword puzzle answers: CAPITALISM, MANIFESTDESTINY, LANDGRANT, BOUNDARY, ENTREPRENEUR, ECONOMY, MASSPRODUCTION, ANNEX, EXPANSION, LATITUDE

ACROSS

2 a system in which privately owned businesses control production

5 the belief that the United States had the right to extend its boundaries from the Atlantic Ocean to the Pacific Ocean

8 a border

9 someone who starts a business, taking all the risks but getting all the profit

10 all the business dealings of a country or state

DOWN

1 public land given by a government

3 to add to something larger or more important

4 the process of making things in large amounts, usually by machine

6 an increase in size

7 the distance north or south of the equator

Tell someone in your family what you have learned about the expanding nation.

LESSON 8

The Road to War

(Student Book pages 46–51)

Lesson Summary Feelings of sectionalism divided the country. The cotton boom brought profit to Southern planters, but it also increased slavery in the South. Many Northerners wanted to abolish slavery. Many also did not want to return fugitive slaves to the South. One goal of the Missouri Compromise was to ban slavery in all territory north of Missouri. When Lincoln became president, radicals in the South believed they could no longer stay in the Union. Southern states voted to secede.

TARGET VOCABULARY

boom a sudden increase in production

abolish to put an end to

abolitionist a person who worked to end slavery

sectionalism loyalty to one's region rather than the whole country

fugitive a person who runs away

Underground Railroad a system of people who helped slaves escape

conductor a person who led slaves to freedom on the Underground Railroad

sue to bring legal action to settle a dispute

radical a person who is in favor of extreme changes

secede to leave one country and form a new one

COGNATES

Spanish-speaking students may find a discussion of the similarities and differences between English and Spanish cognates helpful.

English	Spanish
boom	boom
abolish	abolir
fugitive	fugitivo
conductor	conductor
radical	radical

BEFORE READING

Activate Prior Knowledge

Ask students to tell you what they know about reasons for the Civil War, and write their responses on the board. After you work through the lesson, return to students' ideas and correct them or add to them as necessary.

Introduce Target Vocabulary

Tell students that they are about to read a selection about the road to war. Write the target vocabulary words on the board. Model the pronunciation of each word and have student volunteers repeat the word. Discuss the meaning of each word and, if necessary, write the definition next to the word.

Present Graphic Organizer

Provide each student with a copy of Vocabulary Graphic Organizer: Vocabulary Circle, Teacher Guide page 79. Have students choose a target vocabulary word or assign one to them, and have them write it in the center of the circle. As they read, students should add information about the target vocabulary word to the outer spaces of the circle.

> Word and Definition Cards
> for Lesson 8 are on pages 113 and 114
> of the Teacher Guide.

VOCABULARY STRATEGY: Suffixes

Point out the suffix *-ism* in *sectionalism*. Ask students to name words they know with this suffix. Explain that *-ism* is a suffix that means "a set of ideas or a practice." Note that *sectionalism* is ideas about, as well as the practice of, staying loyal to one's own section of the country rather than to one's country as a whole. Have students look through the Glossary at the back of their book for other words with this suffix.

The Road to War

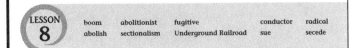

| boom | abolitionist | fugitive | conductor | radical |
| abolish | sectionalism | Underground Railroad | sue | secede |

Changes in technology and transportation did little to change the South. Plantations still remained a way of life. Read this selection to learn how growing cotton indirectly divided the country and led to war.

The Road to War

The Issue of Slavery

Many farmers in South Carolina, Alabama, and Mississippi were cotton planters. They learned that soil planted with cotton year after year wore out. So many of them moved west into Texas. Production suddenly increased from six thousand bales of cotton a year to over two million bales. But the cotton **boom** had a down side. As cotton growing spread west, so did slavery.

A family works in a cotton field.

The Missouri Compromise

By the early 1800s, Northern states had abolished slavery. To **abolish** means to put an end to something. A person who worked to end slavery was called an **abolitionist**. The different views of slavery in the North and the South caused conflict. When Missouri asked to join the Union as a slave state, Northern states objected. Adding a slave state would give the South more power. The Missouri Compromise kept the balance of power. It let in Missouri as a slave state and added Maine as a free state. The plan also banned slavery in all territory north of Missouri.

In the South, feelings of **sectionalism** grew. Some people cared more about their section, or part, of the nation than the nation as a whole. Some Northerners called for an end to slavery in the South. Southerners whose living depended on slavery did not want to make the change. They accused Northerners of trying to destroy the South's economy.

The Underground Railroad

Slaves often ran away to the North. Southerners wanted Northerners to catch and return each **fugitive**, or runaway. Instead, abolitionists set up the **Underground Railroad**. It was a system of people who helped slaves escape. The tracks were not steel. They were back roads and rivers to the North. A **conductor** was a person who led a group to freedom. The conductors were often former slaves.

The Country Breaks Apart

In 1857, Dred Scott, a slave, sued for his freedom. To **sue** is to bring legal action to settle a disagreement. The Supreme Court ruled against him. They said that a slave was not a citizen. They also said that the Missouri Compromise was against the law. That meant that slavery could spread.

In 1860, Abraham Lincoln was elected president. He did not believe in slavery. Radicals in the South believed that the new president and Congress would turn against the South. A **radical** is a person who is in favor of extreme changes. By 1861, eleven Southern states voted to **secede**. They left the United States to form a new nation.

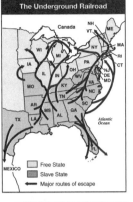
The Underground Railroad

Free State
Slave State
Major routes of escape

Dred Scott sued for his freedom, but the Supreme Court ruled that slaves were not American citizens.

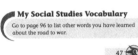
My Social Studies Vocabulary
Go to page 96 to list other words you have learned about the road to war.

DURING READING

Read the selection aloud to students, as they follow along in their books, pausing at the end of each paragraph or section. Review any words or concepts that students are having trouble understanding. Remind students that there is a glossary at the back of their book that contains all of the words that appear in boldfaced type in the lesson.

- Have students name a product for which they think a boom is occurring right now and to give a reason for their opinion.

- Have students identify the relationship between the words *abolish* and *create*. Have them give an example of something they might want to abolish.

- Draw a Venn diagram to compare and contrast a fugitive with a conductor. Have students name similarities and differences.

- Create a *who, what, how, when,* and *why* organizer for the word *secede*. Ask who might secede, and when and why. Elicit the term *radical* and add it to the organizer. Ask what the goal of seceding might be. Ask how the idea of seceding gets started and how it might be carried out.

Have students read the selection again on their own.

AFTER READING

Review Graphic Organizer

Answer any questions students have about the reading selection. Then have students complete or review their graphic organizer and share it with the class.

Summarize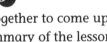

Have students work together to come up with either a written or an oral summary of the lesson. Encourage students to use the target vocabulary words as the basis of their summary. Have students share their summary with the class.

My Social Studies Vocabulary

Encourage students to turn to My Social Studies Vocabulary on page 96 of the student book and use the space provided to add other words about the road to war.

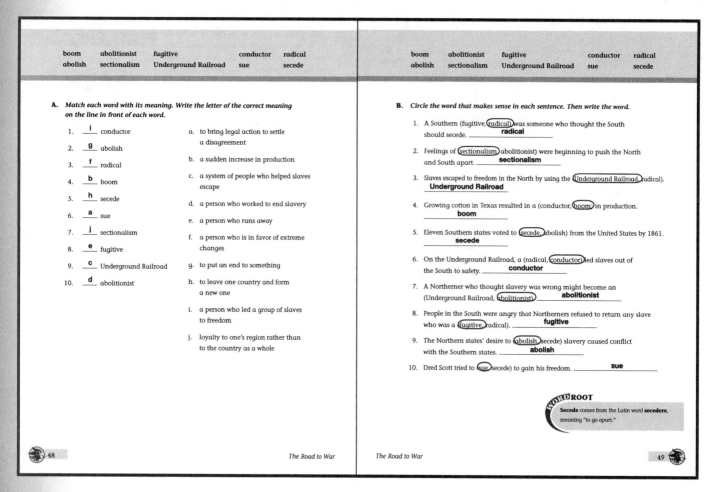

| boom | abolitionist | fugitive | | conductor | radical |
| abolish | sectionalism | Underground Railroad | | sue | secede |

A. Match each word with its meaning. Write the letter of the correct meaning on the line in front of each word.

1. _i_ conductor
2. _g_ abolish
3. _f_ radical
4. _b_ boom
5. _h_ secede
6. _a_ sue
7. _j_ sectionalism
8. _e_ fugitive
9. _c_ Underground Railroad
10. _d_ abolitionist

a. to bring legal action to settle a disagreement
b. a sudden increase in production
c. a system of people who helped slaves escape
d. a person who worked to end slavery
e. a person who runs away
f. a person who is in favor of extreme changes
g. to put an end to something
h. to leave one country and form a new one
i. a person who led a group of slaves to freedom
j. loyalty to one's region rather than to the country as a whole

B. Circle the word that makes sense in each sentence. Then write the word.

1. A Southern (fugitive, **radical**) was someone who thought the South should secede. _____ **radical**
2. Feelings of (**sectionalism**, abolitionist) were beginning to push the North and South apart. _____ **sectionalism**
3. Slaves escaped to freedom in the North by using the (**Underground Railroad**, radical). **Underground Railroad**
4. Growing cotton in Texas resulted in a (conductor, **boom**) in production. _____ **boom**
5. Eleven Southern states voted to (**secede**, abolish) from the United States by 1861. _____ **secede**
6. On the Underground Railroad, a (radical, **conductor**) led slaves out of the South to safety. _____ **conductor**
7. A Northerner who thought slavery was wrong might become an (Underground Railroad, **abolitionist**) _____ **abolitionist**
8. People in the South were angry that Northerners refused to return any slave who was a (**fugitive**, radical). _____ **fugitive**
9. The Northern states' desire to (**abolish**, secede) slavery caused conflict with the Southern states. _____ **abolish**
10. Dred Scott tried to (**sue**, secede) to gain his freedom. _____ **sue**

WORD ROOT
Secede comes from the Latin word **secedere**, meaning "to go apart."

ACTIVITIES A–D

Encourage students to complete as many of the activities as possible. Remind students that they may refer to the Glossary at the back of their book as they complete the activities. Students may work independently, in small groups, or as a class. When students are done, discuss the answers for each activity.

Extensions

These extension ideas allow you to reuse or expand upon the activities. Share them with students who complete the activities before other students, or have students do them for additional practice with target vocabulary words.

A Write the number of syllables in each vocabulary word.

B Rewrite each sentence as a question that can be answered "yes" or "no."

WORD ROOT

Note to students that some roots change when they are used in a different part of speech. Ask students to guess the noun form of the verb *secede*. Their guesses may produce some awkward non-words with typical noun-making suffixes, such as *secedition* or *secedity*. Then tell students that *secession* is the noun form of *secede*. Point out that *secession* is easier to pronounce than some of their guesses, and many noun forms of verbs change their spelling to avoid awkward pronunciation.

C Create a chart with these headings: "Words That Name People"; "Words That Name Practices"; and "Words That Name Actions." Sort the target words into the correct categories.

D Rewrite your sentences, but leave blanks for the vocabulary words. Exchange papers with a partner, and see if you both can fill in the correct words missing from each other's sentences.

boom	abolitionist	fugitive		conductor	radical
abolish	sectionalism	Underground Railroad		sue	secede

C. *Choose the correct vocabulary word to complete each sentence.*

1. The Supreme Court said that a slave was not a citizen and could not ___sue___ for his freedom.

2. More than one ___radical___ was responsible for getting the South to secede from the United States.

3. Over two million bales of cotton were produced each year during the cotton ___boom___ .

4. Southerners decided to ___secede___ after Lincoln became president because they did not believe he shared their interest in keeping slavery.

5. When Northerners rescued fugitive slaves rather than catching and returning them, feelings of ___sectionalism___ increased in the South.

6. The Southern states did not agree with the Northern states' decision to ___abolish___ slavery.

7. Back roads and rivers made up the "tracks" of the ___Underground Railroad___ .

8. Sometimes, a slave who escaped came back to the South to be a ___conductor___ on the Underground Railroad.

9. Ending slavery was the goal of an ___abolitionist___ .

10. The purpose of the Underground Railroad was to help a ___fugitive___ slave escape from the Southern slave states.

---

boom	abolitionist	fugitive		conductor	radical
abolish	sectionalism	Underground Railroad		sue	secede

Students' answers will vary.

D. *Use each word in a sentence that shows you understand the meaning of the word.*

1. abolitionist ___An abolitionist might be a former slave who had gained her freedom in the North.___

2. secede ___Southern states decided to secede from the United States.___

3. sue ___Because a slave was not a citizen, he could not sue his owner for his freedom.___

4. Underground Railroad ___The Underground Railroad helped many slaves find freedom.___

5. fugitive ___A slave became a fugitive in the hope of gaining freedom.___

6. radical ___A radical in the South believed that the South should form its own country.___

7. sectionalism ___Sectionalism in the South divided the country.___

8. abolish ___Plantations in the South had many slaves, so it was hard to abolish slavery there.___

9. boom ___Growing cotton in Texas created a boom in production.___

10. conductor ___A conductor on the Underground Railroad led slaves to freedom.___

Write!

Write your response to the prompt on a separate sheet of paper. Use as many vocabulary words as you can in your writing.

Imagine that you live in the North or the South. Write a letter to a friend or family member, explaining your position on slavery.

Write! ✏️

Provide each student with a copy of Writing Graphic Organizer: Topic Web, Teacher Guide page 80. Tell students to write their position in the upper circle, and use the lower circles to list reasons and explanations.

Sample Answer

Dear Ernestine,

I know you disapprove of my family's practice of slavery. But we need hundreds of workers during this cotton boom. It worries us that you Northerners want to abolish slavery. And not only will you not return our fugitive slaves to us, but you also support the Underground Railroad. I know you view me as a radical, but I support our plans to secede from the United States. I am sorry for our differences.

Your cousin, Millicent

TAKE-HOME ACTIVITY 📖 ✏️ 👄

Assign the Take-Home Activity to students for additional practice with the target vocabulary words. The reproducible Take-Home Activity for Lesson 8 is on page 91 of the Teacher Guide.

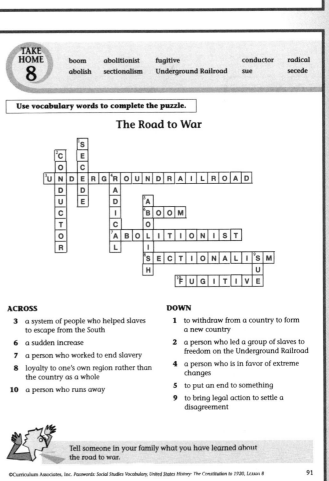

TAKE HOME 8

boom	abolitionist	fugitive		conductor	radical
abolish	sectionalism	Underground Railroad		sue	secede

Use vocabulary words to complete the puzzle.

The Road to War

ACROSS

3 a system of people who helped slaves to escape from the South

6 a sudden increase

7 a person who worked to end slavery

8 loyalty to one's own region rather than the country as a whole

10 a person who runs away

DOWN

1 to withdraw from a country to form a new country

2 a person who led a group of slaves to freedom on the Underground Railroad

4 a person who is in favor of extreme changes

5 to put an end to something

9 to bring legal action to settle a disagreement

Tell someone in your family what you have learned about the road to war.

©Curriculum Associates, Inc. *Passwords: Social Studies Vocabulary, United States History: The Constitution to 1920, Lesson 8*   91

LESSON 9

The Civil War

(Student Book pages 52–57)

Lesson Summary During the Civil War, the Confederacy fought against the Union. When the North invaded the South, the South had to fight a defensive war. Both sides had to draft soldiers to fight. The draft caused riots in the North. One turning point of the war was at Gettysburg. After this battle, the Confederacy could not hope to win the war. Still, the war continued. The South surrendered two years after the Battle of Gettysburg.

TARGET VOCABULARY

civil war a war between groups in the same country

Confederacy the group of Southern states that left the nation

Union the states that remained in the United States

defensive intended to protect against an attack

emancipation the freeing of people

draft to select people for military service

riot a crowd of people who are out of control

turning point an event that changes the way things are going

total war a war against an enemy's civilians and resources as well as its armies

surrender to declare that one's enemy has won and that fighting can stop

COGNATES

Spanish-speaking students may find a discussion of the similarities and differences between English and Spanish cognates helpful.

English	Spanish
civil war	guerra civil
defensive	defensivo
emancipation	emancipación

BEFORE READING

Activate Prior Knowledge

Find out what students already know about the Civil War by creating an alphabetical prediction chart on the board. Make a grid with eight boxes. Label them A–C, D–F, G–I, J–L, M–O, P–R, S–V, and W–Z. Then ask students to name people, places, things, and ideas they already know that are related to the Civil War. Record their answers in the grid; for example, record *Lincoln* in the box labeled J–L. After reading, ask students to add other topics.

Introduce Target Vocabulary

Tell students that they are about to read a selection about the Civil War. Write the target vocabulary words on the board. Model the pronunciation of each word and have student volunteers repeat the word. Discuss the meaning of each word and, if necessary, write the definition next to the word.

Present Graphic Organizer

Provide each student with a copy of Vocabulary Graphic Organizer: Four Square, Teacher Guide page 78. Have each student choose a target vocabulary word or assign a target word to each student. As students read, they should add information about the target vocabulary word to the graphic organizer.

> Word and Definition Cards
> for Lesson 9 are on pages 115 and 116
> of the Teacher Guide.

VOCABULARY STRATEGY: Word Families

Remind students that they can use words in the same word family to help them figure out the meanings of unfamiliar words. For example, students may not know *defensive*, but they may know other words in the same word family, such as *defend* or *defense*. Explain that these words can help them understand that the word *defensive* is related to holding off an attack or fighting back in case of an attack. Students can also learn new words once they learn a single member of a word family. For example, once students learn *emancipation*, they can easily understand the related word *emancipate*.

The Civil War

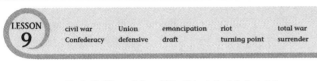

LESSON 9

civil war   Union   emancipation   riot   total war
Confederacy   defensive   draft   turning point   surrender

Was the Civil War worth its costs? Read this selection to find out what happened when Americans went to war against other Americans.

The Civil War

The War Begins

The Civil War split the United States into North and South. A **civil war** is a war between groups in the same country. The group of Southern states that left the nation was called the **Confederacy**. The **Union** was the group of Northern states that remained.

Northerners did not think the Civil War would last long. The Union had more people to serve in the army. It had more factories to build weapons and more railroads to transport soldiers. Its ships could block Southern ports to stop trade with Europe.

The Confederacy, however, had strong military leaders, such as General Robert E. Lee. And its soldiers were well trained. Also, the South was mostly fighting a **defensive** war on its own land. It did everything it could to protect against attack.

Southern States Secede

Can you name the states that left the Union?

The Emancipation of the Slaves

The North had gone to war to unite the country. Its goal was not to end slavery. But in 1863, President Lincoln freed all slaves in the Southern states that had left the Union. Lincoln hoped that the **emancipation**, or freeing, of the slaves would weaken the South and help end the war.

President Lincoln says slaves in Confederate states are free.

War Takes Its Toll

When the war began in 1861, soldiers on both sides signed up eagerly. Soon, however, people lost hope. Both sides had to draft soldiers. To **draft** means to choose someone from a group to serve in the armed forces. In the North, riots broke out. A **riot** is a crowd of people who become out of control.

African Americans did not need to be drafted into the Union army — they wanted to serve.

The Confederacy won many battles in the early years of the war. The Battle of Gettysburg, in 1863, marked a **turning point**, or major change. The Confederate army attacked but lost. Never again would it have the strength to invade the North.

The Battle of Gettysburg was a turning point in the Civil War.

Victory for the North

In the end, the North won the Civil War. One reason was its practice of **total war**. The North attacked civilians and resources as well as the army. Anything useful to the enemy, such as food, buildings, and equipment, was destroyed. In April 1865, the Southern army surrendered. To **surrender** means to declare that an enemy has won and that fighting can stop. The Civil War ended with more than 600,000 dead.

My Social Studies Vocabulary

Go to page 96 to list other words you have learned about the Civil War.

52   *The Civil War*   *The Civil War*   53

DURING READING

Read the selection aloud to students, as they follow along in their books, pausing at the end of each paragraph or section. Review any words or concepts that students are having trouble understanding. Remind students that there is a glossary at the back of their book that contains all of the words that appear in boldfaced type in the lesson.

- Explain to students that adding a suffix to a word often changes a word's part of speech. Adding *-ion, -tion,* or *-ation* changes a verb to a noun. Have students identify the target vocabulary word with the suffix *-ation* (*emancipation*). Have students form the verb of the word (*emancipate*). Point out the spelling changes.

- Draw a Venn diagram on the board and label the circles *Union* and *Confederacy.* Have students supply details to complete the organizer.

- Have students explain the relationship between the draft and a riot in the North. Draw a simple cause-and-effect organizer to show their answer. Ask what happens in a riot.

Have students read the selection again on their own.

AFTER READING

Review Graphic Organizer

Answer any questions students have about the reading selection. Then have students complete or review their graphic organizer and share it with the class.

Summarize

Have students work together to come up with either a written or an oral summary of the lesson. Encourage students to use the target vocabulary words as the basis of their summary. Have students share their summary with the class.

My Social Studies Vocabulary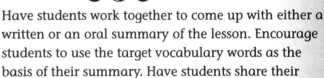

Encourage students to turn to My Social Studies Vocabulary on page 96 of the student book and use the space provided to add other words about the Civil War.

The Civil War

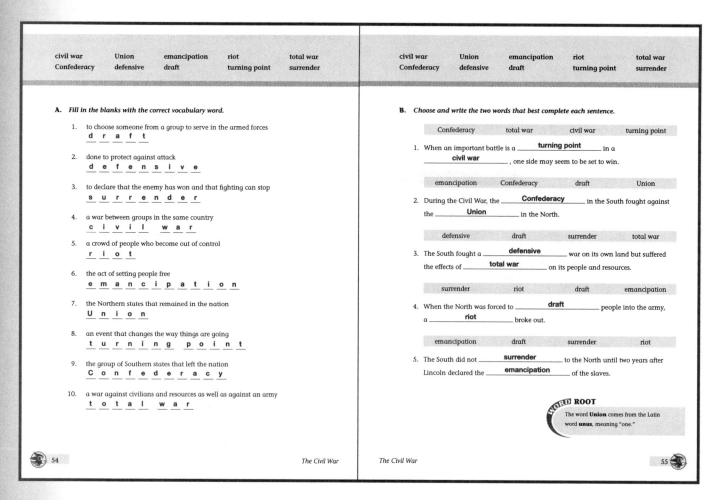

civil war   Union   emancipation   riot   total war
Confederacy   defensive   draft   turning point   surrender

A. Fill in the blanks with the correct vocabulary word.

1. to choose someone from a group to serve in the armed forces
   d r a f t

2. done to protect against attack
   d e f e n s i v e

3. to declare that the enemy has won and that fighting can stop
   s u r r e n d e r

4. a war between groups in the same country
   c i v i l   w a r

5. a crowd of people who become out of control
   r i o t

6. the act of setting people free
   e m a n c i p a t i o n

7. the Northern states that remained in the nation
   U n i o n

8. an event that changes the way things are going
   t u r n i n g   p o i n t

9. the group of Southern states that left the nation
   C o n f e d e r a c y

10. a war against civilians and resources as well as against an army
    t o t a l   w a r

54   The Civil War

civil war   Union   emancipation   riot   total war
Confederacy   defensive   draft   turning point   surrender

B. Choose and write the two words that best complete each sentence.

Confederacy   total war   civil war   turning point

1. When an important battle is a ___turning point___ in a ___civil war___, one side may seem to be set to win.

emancipation   Confederacy   draft   Union

2. During the Civil War, the ___Confederacy___ in the South fought against the ___Union___ in the North.

defensive   draft   surrender   total war

3. The South fought a ___defensive___ war on its own land but suffered the effects of ___total war___ on its people and resources.

surrender   riot   draft   emancipation

4. When the North was forced to ___draft___ people into the army, a ___riot___ broke out.

emancipation   draft   surrender   riot

5. The South did not ___surrender___ to the North until two years after Lincoln declared the ___emancipation___ of the slaves.

WORD ROOT
The word **Union** comes from the Latin word *unus*, meaning "one."

The Civil War   55

ACTIVITIES A–D

Encourage students to complete as many of the activities as possible. Remind students that they may refer to the Glossary at the back of their book as they complete the activities. Students may work independently, in small groups, or as a class. When students are done, discuss the answers for each activity.

Extensions

These extension ideas allow you to reuse or expand upon the activities. Share them with students who complete the activities before other students, or have students do them for additional practice with target vocabulary words.

A Write the number of syllables in each word.

B After you have chosen the correct answers for each sentence, explain why the wrong answers did not make sense in the sentence.

WORD ROOT

Have students decide how the spellings and meanings of the following words relate to their common Latin root *unus: unify, unique, uniform, unit, unite,* and *universe.*

C Draw a diagram showing how any two target words are related. For example, you might use a diagram to show how one thing led to or caused another, or how one or more words fall into a category named by another word.

D Choose two of the target words and write a single sentence that uses them both correctly.

C. *Choose the correct vocabulary word to complete each sentence.*

1. President Lincoln hoped that the __emancipation__ of the slaves would weaken the South.

2. Angry Northerners started a __riot__ when they learned that they might be drafted into the armed forces.

3. The practice of __total war__ against the South was successful because it affected all its people and resources, not just its army.

4. The Southern states of the __Confederacy__ seceded from the nation to defend their way of life.

5. When two groups within the same country strongly disagree about something, the result could be a __civil war__ .

6. When there are not enough soldiers to fight a war, a government might have to __draft__ people.

7. The South was forced to fight a __defensive__ war to protect its land and people.

8. The original goal of the __Union__ was to unite the country again.

9. Winning the Battle of Gettysburg was a __turning point__ for the North, which had lost many earlier battles.

10. The Civil War ended when the Southern army decided to __surrender__ .

56   The Civil War

Students' answers will vary.

D. *Use each word in a sentence that shows you understand the meaning of the word.*

1. emancipation __Lincoln's emancipation of slaves in the Confederacy angered white Southerners.__

2. surrender __The defeated Confederacy had to surrender to the Union.__

3. civil war __A civil war divides a country against itself.__

4. riot __Angry Northerners who did not want to go to war started a riot.__

5. Confederacy __The Confederacy was made up of Southern states that had left the United States.__

6. total war __A total war destroys the lives of civilians as well as soldiers.__

7. Union __The Northern states were called the Union.__

8. defensive __The South fought a defensive war, trying to resist the North's attacks.__

9. turning point __One turning point of the Civil War was the Battle of Gettysburg.__

10. draft __The North and South did not have enough soldiers, so they had to draft them.__

Write!

Write your response to the prompt on a separate sheet of paper. Use as many vocabulary words as you can in your writing.

Suppose the Civil War has just ended. How would people living in the North and those living in the South differ in their views of the war?

The Civil War   57

Write!

Provide each student with a copy of Writing Graphic Organizer: Two-Column Chart, Teacher Guide page 83. Tell students to label one column "North" and the other column "South." In each column they can write down how the two parts of the country might view the war.

Sample Answer

    After the Civil War, both Northerners and Southerners probably felt that the war was a waste. Even though slavery was abolished, many Union soldiers died and families lost loved ones. Southerners not only lost soldiers in battle; their food, buildings, and equipment were destroyed by the Union army's practice of total war. Some Southerners probably wished that the South had not seceded from the Union, but most probably felt as if they had no choice.

TAKE-HOME ACTIVITY

Assign the Take-Home Activity to students for additional practice with the target vocabulary words. The reproducible Take-Home Activity for Lesson 9 is on page 92 of the Teacher Guide.

TAKE HOME 9

Use vocabulary words to complete the puzzle.

The Civil War

[Crossword puzzle]

ACROSS

4 a major change

6 a war between groups in the same country

7 the group of Southern states that left the nation

9 the act of setting people free

10 a crowd of people who become out of control

DOWN

1 done to protect against attack

2 the practice of attacking the enemy's civilians and resources as well as the army

3 to declare that an enemy has won and that fighting can stop

5 the nation, or the Northern states, after the South left the nation

8 to choose someone from a group to serve in the armed forces

Tell someone in your family what you have learned about the Civil War.

LESSON 10

Reconstruction

(Student Book pages 58–63)

TARGET VOCABULARY

assassination the killing of a public figure

Reconstruction a time of rebuilding the South after the Civil War

freedmen former slaves

sharecropper a farmer who works someone else's land in return for a share of the crop

tenant farmer someone who rents land to farm

black codes laws passed by Southern states to limit the rights of freedmen

inherit to get something from someone after he or she has died

segregation the practice of separating people by race

carpetbagger a Northerner who moved to the South during Reconstruction

scalawag a Southern white who was in favor of Reconstruction

COGNATES

Spanish-speaking students may find a discussion of the similarities and differences between English and Spanish cognates helpful.

English	Spanish
assassination	asesinato
Reconstruction	Reconstrucción
segregation	segregación

Lesson Summary Before his assassination, Lincoln had made plans for Reconstruction, but he did not live to see it. Although freedmen had new rights, Southern states passed black codes to limit those rights. They also practiced segregation. Reconstruction was a time of great tension. Some Southern whites disliked the Northerners who came south. They called them carpetbaggers. They also disliked Southerners who supported Reconstruction and called them scalawags.

BEFORE READING

Activate Prior Knowledge

Explain that this lesson is about the period after the Civil War. Write each target vocabulary word on the board, ask students to copy it, and have students rate their knowledge of it by deciding whether they know it, have some idea of what it means, or don't know it. After reading, return to this list and have students rate their knowledge again.

Introduce Target Vocabulary

Tell students that they are about to read a selection about Reconstruction. Model the pronunciation of each target vocabulary word and have student volunteers repeat the word. Discuss the meaning of each word and, if necessary, write the definition next to the word.

Present Graphic Organizer

Provide each student with a copy of Vocabulary Graphic Organizer: Four Square, Teacher Guide page 78. Have each student choose a target vocabulary word or assign a target word to each student. As students read, they should add information about the target vocabulary word to the graphic organizer.

> Word and Definition Cards for Lesson 10 are on pages 117 and 118 of the Teacher Guide.

VOCABULARY STRATEGY: Compound Words

Remind students that a compound word is a single term that is made up of two or more words. Sometimes the words form a closed compound word, which has no space between the words, such as *girlfriend*. Sometimes the words form an open compound word, which has a space between the words, such as *space race*. Have students find all the compound target words that are open or closed compounds (*freedmen, sharecropper, tenant farmer, black codes,* and *carpetbagger*). Work with students to identify the words that make up each compound word, and talk about how the individual words give clues to each target word's meaning.

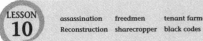

LESSON 10

assassination   freedmen   tenant farmer   inherit   carpetbagger
Reconstruction sharecropper   black codes   segregation   scalawag

During Reconstruction, the government worked to rebuild the South and to bring it back into the Union. How do you think Southerners felt about the changes that were happening? Read this selection to find out.

Reconstruction

Reconstruction and President Lincoln

The Thirteenth Amendment ended slavery in 1865. But President Lincoln never got a chance to see the change. The law passed just after his assassination. An **assassination** is the killing of a public figure. Lincoln had hoped to rebuild the South and bring it back into the United States. This plan was called **Reconstruction**. It happened without him.

The State of the South

The South lay in ruins. Cities and railroads were destroyed. A way of life was gone. Nearly forty million **freedmen**, former slaves, had no jobs or education. Many became sharecroppers. A **sharecropper** is a farmer who works someone else's land in return for a share of the crop. Sharecroppers made hardly enough to live on. Other freedmen became tenant farmers. A **tenant farmer** pays rent to work someone else's land.

A sharecropper worked very hard but stayed poor.

Southern Actions

Southern states wanted to limit the rights that freedmen had gained. So they passed laws called **black codes**. The laws said that freedmen could not vote, carry guns, or work skilled jobs. They could not own or inherit property. **Inherit** means to get something from someone after he or she has died.

Southern states also passed laws that separated people by race. This practice is called **segregation**. African Americans could not go to the same public places as whites.

Reconstruction Problems

In parts of the South, there was little law. A group calling itself the Ku Klux Klan formed. They claimed their goal was to bring law and order. But they worked against the goals of Reconstruction. They tried to strike fear into African Americans who dared to claim their rights.

Many Northerners moved to the South during Reconstruction. Some went to help. Others went to make money. These people often carried their things in bags made of carpet. Southerners called such a person a **carpetbagger**. Some Southerners disliked carpetbaggers. They also disliked scalawags. A **scalawag** was a Southern white person who was in favor of Reconstruction.

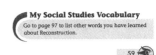
Some Southerners viewed carpetbaggers as greedy robbers.

In 1877, Reconstruction ended. The results were mixed. The North and the South were one country again. New amendments gave African Americans full rights, including the right to vote. Still, it would take almost a full century before African Americans would actually enjoy those rights.

My Social Studies Vocabulary
Go to page 97 to list other words you have learned about Reconstruction.

DURING READING

Read the selection aloud to students, as they follow along in their books, pausing at the end of each paragraph or section. Review any words or concepts that students are having trouble understanding. Remind students that there is a glossary at the back of their book that contains all of the words that appear in boldfaced type in the lesson.

- Ask students to find the base word *construct* in Reconstruction. Point out that *construct* means "to build." Note that *re-* means "again." Explain that Reconstruction was a period of rebuilding.

- Draw a Venn diagram and label the two circles *sharecropper* and *tenant farmer*. Have students identify one thing to write in each of the two circles and one thing to write in the overlapping area.

- Tell students that before the Civil War, *scalawag* referred to a good-for-nothing person, a rascal. In modern times, the word is used to convey its original meaning and has nothing to do with politics.

Have students read the selection again on their own.

AFTER READING

Review Graphic Organizer

Answer any questions students have about the reading selection. Then have students complete or review their graphic organizer and share it with the class.

Summarize

Have students work together to come up with either a written or an oral summary of the lesson. Encourage students to use the target vocabulary words as the basis of their summary. Have students share their summary with the class.

My Social Studies Vocabulary

Encourage students to turn to My Social Studies Vocabulary on page 97 of the student book and use the space provided to add other words about the Reconstruction.

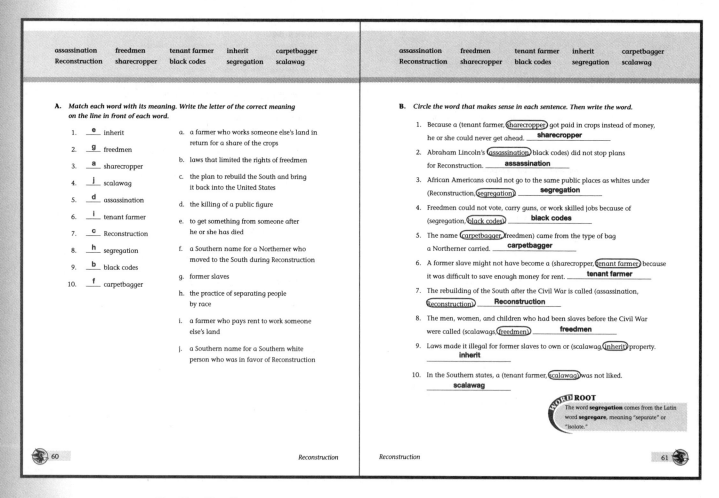

A. Match each word with its meaning. Write the letter of the correct meaning on the line in front of each word.

1. __e__ inherit
2. __g__ freedmen
3. __a__ sharecropper
4. __j__ scalawag
5. __d__ assassination
6. __i__ tenant farmer
7. __c__ Reconstruction
8. __h__ segregation
9. __b__ black codes
10. __f__ carpetbagger

a. a farmer who works someone else's land in return for a share of the crops
b. laws that limited the rights of freedmen
c. the plan to rebuild the South and bring it back into the United States
d. the killing of a public figure
e. to get something from someone after he or she has died
f. a Southern name for a Northerner who moved to the South during Reconstruction
g. former slaves
h. the practice of separating people by race
i. a farmer who pays rent to work someone else's land
j. a Southern name for a Southern white person who was in favor of Reconstruction

B. Circle the word that makes sense in each sentence. Then write the word.

1. Because a (tenant farmer, *sharecropper*) got paid in crops instead of money, he or she could never get ahead. __sharecropper__
2. Abraham Lincoln's (*assassination*, black codes) did not stop plans for Reconstruction. __assassination__
3. African Americans could not go to the same public places as whites under (Reconstruction, *segregation*). __segregation__
4. Freedmen could not vote, carry guns, or work skilled jobs because of (segregation, *black codes*). __black codes__
5. The name (*carpetbagger*, freedmen) came from the type of bag a Northerner carried. __carpetbagger__
6. A former slave might not have become a (sharecropper, *tenant farmer*) because it was difficult to save enough money for rent. __tenant farmer__
7. The rebuilding of the South after the Civil War is called (assassination, *Reconstruction*). __Reconstruction__
8. The men, women, and children who had been slaves before the Civil War were called (scalawags, *freedmen*). __freedmen__
9. Laws made it illegal for former slaves to own or (scalawag, *inherit*) property. __inherit__
10. In the Southern states, a (tenant farmer, *scalawag*) was not liked. __scalawag__

WORD ROOT
The word **segregation** comes from the Latin word **segregare**, meaning "separate" or "isolate."

ACTIVITIES A–D

Encourage students to complete as many of the activities as possible. Remind students that they may refer to the Glossary at the back of their book as they complete the activities. Students may work independently, in small groups, or as a class. When students are done, discuss the answers for each activity.

Extensions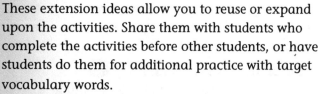

These extension ideas allow you to reuse or expand upon the activities. Share them with students who complete the activities before other students, or have students do them for additional practice with target vocabulary words.

A Look up two of the target vocabulary words in the Glossary, in a dictionary, and in an encyclopedia. How are the definitions similar? How are they different?

B Make a chart with two columns. Label the columns "Words That Name People," and "Words That Name Things." Write the target words in the correct column of the chart.

C Write five target words that have a word part (prefix, suffix, root word, or base word) that is familiar to you. Underline the word part. Next to the word target word, write another word you know with the same word part.

D Combine any two of the sentences you wrote into a single sentence. Cut or add words as needed so that your combined sentence makes sense and reads clearly.

WORD ROOT

Ask students what part of speech *segregation* is (*noun*). Ask students what the verb form and the adjective form of *segregation* are (*segregate* and *segregated*). Challenge students to come up with the word that means the opposite of *segregation* (*integration*).

assassination   freedmen   tenant farmer   inherit   carpetbagger
Reconstruction   sharecropper   black codes   segregation   scalawag

C. *Choose the correct vocabulary word to complete each sentence.*

1. President Lincoln's _____**assassination**_____ occurred before Reconstruction.

2. It was difficult for African American families to get wealthy because they could not _____**inherit**_____ property.

3. If someone from the South favored Reconstruction but was not a former slave, that person was called a _____**scalawag**_____ .

4. The Thirteenth Amendment freed African Americans, but laws known as _____**black codes**_____ took away many of their rights.

5. If someone could afford to pay rent to farm land, that person became a _____**tenant farmer**_____ .

6. Without a job or education, _____**freedmen**_____ were not much better off than they had been as slaves.

7. An African-American farmer was more likely to be a _____**sharecropper**_____ than a tenant farmer.

8. Some Southerners thought that a _____**carpetbagger**_____ from the North came only to make money.

9. The years between 1865 and 1877 were the time of _____**Reconstruction**_____ .

10. Black codes and _____**segregation**_____ kept African Americans in the South from gaining their rights.

62   *Reconstruction*

---

assassination   freedmen   tenant farmer   inherit   carpetbagger
Reconstruction   sharecropper   black codes   segregation   scalawag

Students' answers will vary.

D. *Use each word in a sentence that shows you understand the meaning of the word.*

1. assassination **The assassination of President Lincoln happened before Reconstruction.**

2. inherit **The man hoped to inherit the family business.**

3. black codes **Black codes took away African Americans' rights.**

4. freedmen **Freedmen were not much better off than slaves.**

5. scalawag **Many Southerners felt that scalawags were siding against them.**

6. tenant farmer **A tenant farmer needed money to rent land.**

7. Reconstruction **The purpose of Reconstruction was to make the Union whole again.**

8. carpetbagger **A carpetbagger hoped to make easy money in the South.**

9. segregation **Segregation continued to keep races apart.**

10. sharecropper **A sharecropper had to give part of his crop to the landowner.**

Write!

Write your response to the prompt on a separate sheet of paper. Use as many vocabulary words as you can in your writing.

Do you think that Reconstruction was a success or a failure? Explain why you think so.

Reconstruction   *63*

Write!

Provide each student with a copy of Writing Graphic Organizer: Main Idea and Details Chart, Teacher Guide page 82. Tell students to write the main ideas they want to make about Reconstruction in the main idea boxes. Then have them use the details boxes to list the information they will use to support their main ideas.

Sample Answer

Reconstruction was not the success Lincoln probably thought it would be. White Southerners wanted to rebuild their lives, but they did not like being forced to make political changes. They also did not like the presence of Northern carpetbaggers. Reconstruction did not improve the lives of black Southerners very much. Slaves were now freedmen, but Southern states passed black codes that limited their new freedom and enforced segregation. Freedmen also had little chance of bettering their lives because being a sharecropper was the only work they could get.

TAKE-HOME ACTIVITY

Assign the Take-Home Activity to students for additional practice with the target vocabulary words. The reproducible Take-Home Activity for Lesson 10 is on page 93 of the Teacher Guide.

TAKE HOME 10

assassination   freedmen   tenant farmer   inherit   carpetbagger
Reconstruction   sharecropper   black codes   segregation   scalawag

Use vocabulary words to complete the puzzle.

Reconstruction

ACROSS

4 to get something from someone after her or she has died

7 a Northerner who went to the South during Reconstruction

8 the killing of a public figure

9 the plan to rebuild the South and bring it back into the Union

10 a farmer who works someone else's land in return for a share of the crop

DOWN

1 the practice of separating people by race

2 a Southern white person who was in favor of Reconstruction

3 a farmer who pays rent to work someone else's land

5 former slaves

6 laws that limited the rights of freedmen

Tell someone in your family what you have learned about Reconstruction.

Reconstruction

LESSON 11
Industrialization

(Student Book pages 64–69)

TARGET VOCABULARY

industrialization the change from being a society based on farming to being a society based on industry

invention an original idea for a new process or product

transcontinental across an entire continent

corporation a business owned by many people, each of whom own shares

regulate to control

monopoly a company that controls an entire industry

sweatshop a small factory or mill with poor working conditions

labor union a group of workers who join together to bring changes

strike a stopping of work to try to force changes for the better

panic a time when businesses fail, jobs disappear, and banks close

COGNATES

Spanish-speaking students may find a discussion of the similarities and differences between English and Spanish cognates helpful.

English	Spanish
industrialization	industrialización
invention	invención
regulate	regular
monopoly	monopolio

VOCABULARY STRATEGY: Using Pictures

Explain to students that illustrations and photographs in textbooks can help them to understand unfamiliar words. Point out to students the pictures on pages 64–65—a photograph of the first transcontinental rail line, a cartoon of a monopoly, and the photograph of striking workers. Remind students to refer to pictures as they read to get a better understanding of new words.

Lesson Summary Industrialization changed life in the United States. Demand for new inventions created a need for new factories. A new process for making steel led to more railroads. In 1869, a transcontinental railroad joined the East and the West. Large corporations began to replace small companies. Eventually laws were needed to regulate corporations and prevent monopolies. Labor unions were created to protect the rights of workers and discourage sweatshops. Businesses also experienced panics during which jobs disappeared.

BEFORE READING

Activate Prior Knowledge
Lead students in a discussion of how large industries, such as the transportation industry, the electronics industry, and the food industry, affect how people live today. Tell students that at one time, instead of big factories, there were mostly small farms and small businesses. Ask them to think about the ways in which factories with machines and many employees likely changed life for people living in the United States.

Introduce Target Vocabulary
Tell students they are about to read a selection about industrialization in the United States. Write the target vocabulary words on the board. Model the pronunciation of each word and have student volunteers repeat the word. Discuss the meaning of each word and, if necessary, write the definition next to the word.

Present Graphic Organizer
Provide each student with a copy of Vocabulary Graphic Organizer: Vocabulary Map, Teacher Guide page 77. Have students choose or assign each student a target vocabulary word. Students should write the target vocabulary word in the center box of the Vocabulary Map. As students read the lesson, they should complete the graphic organizer.

> Word and Definition Cards for Lesson 11 are on pages 119 and 120 of the Teacher Guide.

Industrialization

LESSON 11

industrialization · transcontinental · regulate · sweatshop · strike
invention · corporation · monopoly · labor union · panic

Machines play an important part in modern life. Could new machines change how you live? Could they change an entire country? Read this selection to learn how machines changed life in the United States after the Civil War.

Industrialization

During the 1800s, many people stopped farming for a living. Instead, they made goods in factories. A new age of industry began. Industry is the making of goods in a factory. The change to industry from farming is called **industrialization**.

Inventions

There were many new inventions during the 1800s. An **invention** is an original idea for making new things. Some inventions led to new products. Others improved how goods were made.

In the 1850s, a new process for making steel was developed. It helped lead to more railroads. In the West, thousands of workers were brought from China to help lay tracks. In 1869, a railroad joined the East and the West for the first time. It was a **transcontinental** railroad. It went across the whole continent.

The eastern tracks and the western tracks of the transcontinental railroad met in Utah.

Big Business Grows

In the early days of the nation, businesses were small. Often, they had just one owner. In the late 1800s, a new kind of business began. It was the corporation. A **corporation** is a business owned by many people. Each person owns a part, or share, of a business.

At first, there were few laws to **regulate**, or control, corporations. They could do what they wanted. For example, in the late 1800s, one oil company got bigger and bigger. It put other oil companies out of business. Finally, it became a **monopoly**. It controlled the whole industry.

This cartoon shows Standard Oil, a monopoly, crushing other businesses.

Labor Unions

Many people worked in sweatshops. A **sweatshop** is a small factory or mill with poor working conditions. People worked long hours—sometimes as many as 16 hours a day—for low pay. Children often worked in sweatshops, too.

Workers joined together to fight back. They formed labor unions. A **labor union** is a group of workers who join together to bring changes. Often, labor unions use a strike to get what they want. During a **strike**, people stop working to get higher pay or better conditions. Some strikes ended in bloodshed between workers and factory owners' "strike breakers."

What did these striking workers want?

Hard Times

Business did not always do well. In 1873 and 1893, panics occurred. During a **panic**, businesses fail. Jobs disappear, banks close, and families go hungry. People wondered why the government wasn't doing more to control business.

My Social Studies Vocabulary
Go to page 97 to list other words you have learned about industrialization.

DURING READING

Read the selection aloud to students, as they follow along in their books, pausing at the end of each paragraph or section. Review any words or concepts that students are having trouble understanding. Remind students that there is a glossary at the back of their book that contains all of the words that appear in boldfaced type in the lesson.

- Tell students that *transcontinental* incorporates the common Latin prefix *trans-*, meaning "across." Challenge students to brainstorm a list of other words that use this prefix. Have them check their responses in a dictionary and connect their definitions to the meaning of *transcontinental*.

- Explain to students that the Greek word *monos* means "single, alone." Ask students which target vocabulary word contains the Greek root word *monos* (*monopoly*). Challenge them to explain how its meaning relates to the root word (*a monopoly refers to a single company dominating a market*).

- Divide the class into small groups. Have students in each group take on the role of either workers in the 1800s fighting for better working conditions or representatives of a corporation. Have each group give a short speech that incorporates at least three target vocabulary words.

Have students read the selection again on their own.

AFTER READING

Review Graphic Organizer

Answer any questions students have about the reading selection. Then have students complete or review their graphic organizer and share it with the class.

Summarize

Have students work together to come up with either a written or an oral summary of the lesson. Encourage students to use the target vocabulary words as the basis of their summary. Have students share their summary with the class.

My Social Studies Vocabulary

Encourage students to turn to My Social Studies Vocabulary on page 97 of the student book and use the space provided to add other words related to industrialization.

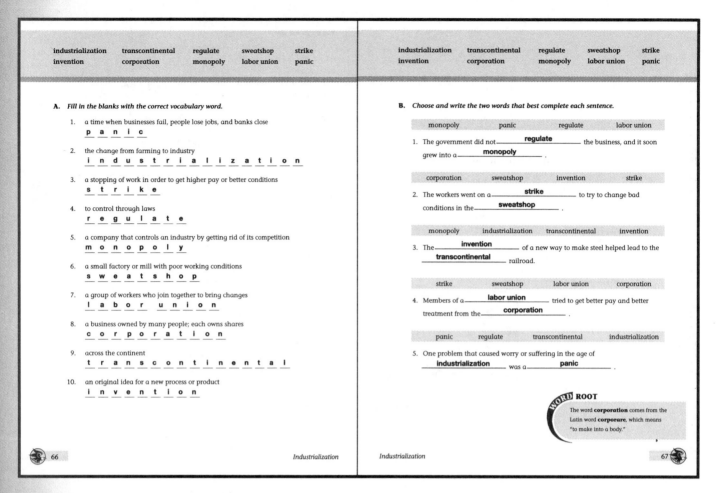

Page 66

industrialization   transcontinental   regulate   sweatshop   strike
invention   corporation   monopoly   labor union   panic

A. *Fill in the blanks with the correct vocabulary word.*

1. a time when businesses fail, people lose jobs, and banks close
   p a n i c

2. the change from farming to industry
   i n d u s t r i a l i z a t i o n

3. a stopping of work in order to get higher pay or better conditions
   s t r i k e

4. to control through laws
   r e g u l a t e

5. a company that controls an industry by getting rid of its competition
   m o n o p o l y

6. a small factory or mill with poor working conditions
   s w e a t s h o p

7. a group of workers who join together to bring changes
   l a b o r   u n i o n

8. a business owned by many people; each owns shares
   c o r p o r a t i o n

9. across the continent
   t r a n s c o n t i n e n t a l

10. an original idea for a new process or product
    i n v e n t i o n

66   *Industrialization*

Page 67

industrialization   transcontinental   regulate   sweatshop   strike
invention   corporation   monopoly   labor union   panic

B. *Choose and write the two words that best complete each sentence.*

| monopoly | panic | regulate | labor union |

1. The government did not _____**regulate**_____ the business, and it soon grew into a _____**monopoly**_____ .

| corporation | sweatshop | invention | strike |

2. The workers went on a _____**strike**_____ to try to change bad conditions in the _____**sweatshop**_____ .

| monopoly | industrialization | transcontinental | invention |

3. The _____**invention**_____ of a new way to make steel helped lead to the _____**transcontinental**_____ railroad.

| strike | sweatshop | labor union | corporation |

4. Members of a _____**labor union**_____ tried to get better pay and better treatment from the _____**corporation**_____ .

| panic | regulate | transcontinental | industrialization |

5. One problem that caused worry or suffering in the age of _____**industrialization**_____ was a _____**panic**_____ .

WORD ROOT
The word **corporation** comes from the Latin word **corporare**, which means "to make into a body."

Industrialization   67

ACTIVITIES A–D

Encourage students to complete as many of the activities as possible. Remind students that they may refer to the Glossary at the back of their book as they complete the activities. Students may work independently, in small groups, or as a class. When students are done, discuss the answers for each activity.

Extensions

These extension ideas allow you to reuse or expand upon the activities. Share them with students who complete the activities before other students, or have students do them for additional practice with target vocabulary words.

A Put the target vocabulary words in alphabetical order.

B Underline the nouns and circle the verbs in each sentence.

C Rewrite each sentence as a question that can be answered with "yes" or "no."

D Go to the Internet to find a picture, diagram, or an additional detail to go with each sentence.

WORD ROOT

Discuss with students how the meaning of the target word *corporation* relates to the Latin root *corporare*. (*In a corporation, investors come together to create one "body," or organization.*) Tell students that a related word is *corps,* which is a body of people acting together or with a similar purpose—such as an *army corps* or the *press corps*. Note that the *ps* in *corps* is not pronounced.

| industrialization | transcontinental | regulate | sweatshop | strike |
| invention | corporation | monopoly | labor union | panic |

C. *Choose the correct vocabulary word to complete each sentence.*

1. The _____**transcontinental**_____ railroad reached from the East to the West.

2. One company had a _____**monopoly**_____ on the whole oil business.

3. Because businesses failed, people lost their jobs during a _____**panic**_____ .

4. A new factory was built to produce the new _____**invention**_____ .

5. Many people own part of a business in a _____**corporation**_____ .

6. Adults and children worked side by side in the dirty _____**sweatshop**_____ .

7. The workers went on a _____**strike**_____ to try to shorten their workday.

8. People made many goods in factories during the age of _____**industrialization**_____ .

9. The corporation did what it wanted because the government did not _____**regulate**_____ it.

10. The factory workers joined to form a _____**labor union**_____ .

| industrialization | transcontinental | regulate | sweatshop | strike |
| invention | corporation | monopoly | labor union | panic |

Students' answers will vary.

D. *Use each word in a sentence that shows you know the meaning of the word.*

1. strike **The workers did not go to work during the strike.**

2. panic **The banks closed during the panic.**

3. labor union **The labor union fought for a shorter workday.**

4. industrialization **Industrialization caused many people to leave the family farm.**

5. sweatshop **Even children worked long hours in the sweatshop.**

6. transcontinental **The transcontinental railroad crossed the country.**

7. regulate **Laws did not regulate the corporations, so they did what they wanted.**

8. invention **One important invention was a new way to make steel.**

9. corporation **A person can own one or many shares in a corporation.**

10. monopoly **When other companies went out of business, one company had a monopoly.**

 Write!
Write your response to the prompt on a separate sheet of paper. Use as many vocabulary words as you can in your writing.

Describe some of the changes that occurred in the United States as a result of industrialization.

Write!

Distribute Writing Graphic Organizer: Main Idea and Details Chart, Teacher Guide page 82. In each Main Idea box, students should write about one change that occurred in the United States during the age of industrialization. In the corresponding Details box, they should write details about this change and its importance.

Sample Answer

During the time of industrialization, people began to work in factories instead of on farms. New inventions led to improvements in how things were made. A new way to make steel led to the transcontinental railroad.

During the time of industrialization, many corporations were formed. Some corporations became monopolies. Some workers had to work in sweatshops. Labor unions sometimes used strikes to get better pay or better working conditions.

TAKE-HOME ACTIVITY

Assign the Take-Home Activity to students for additional practice with the target vocabulary words. The reproducible Take-Home Activity for Lesson 11 is on page 94 of the Teacher Guide.

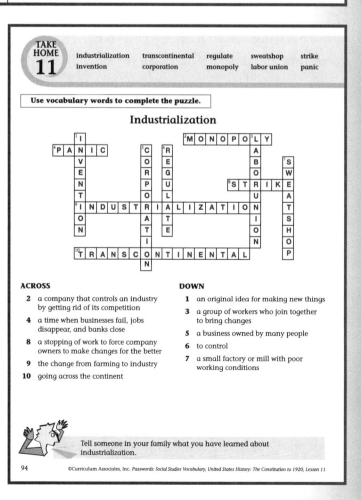

TAKE HOME 11

| industrialization | transcontinental | regulate | sweatshop | strike |
| invention | corporation | monopoly | labor union | panic |

Use vocabulary words to complete the puzzle.

Industrialization

ACROSS
2 a company that controls an industry by getting rid of its competition
4 a time when businesses fail, jobs disappear, and banks close
8 a stopping of work to force company owners to make changes for the better
9 the change from farming to industry
10 going across the continent

DOWN
1 an original idea for making new things
3 a group of workers who join together to bring changes
5 a business owned by many people
6 to control
7 a small factory or mill with poor working conditions

Tell someone in your family what you have learned about industrialization.

94   ©Curriculum Associates, Inc. *Passwords: Social Studies Vocabulary, United States History: The Constitution to 1920, Lesson 11*

LESSON 12

The Growth of Cities

(Student Book pages 70–75)

Lesson Summary In the 1800s, cities in the United States grew and changed. One reason for this was urbanization due to industrialization. Another reason was immigration. Often immigrants were fleeing poverty in their homelands. Housing became a problem in cities, with many immigrants living in slums and tenements. Other changes in cities included the appearance of skyscrapers and the use of electric streetcars. Streetcars allowed people to commute to cities from the suburbs.

TARGET VOCABULARY

urbanization the growth of cities

immigrant a person who comes to a new country to live

emigration leaving a country to live in a different country

nativism the practice or policy of favoring native-born people over immigrants

slum a poor, crowded part of a city

tenement a crowded apartment house in the poor part of a city

ethnic group people related by customs, language, culture, or country of origin

skyscraper a very tall building

suburb an area just outside the city limits

commute the trip back and forth to work

COGNATES

Spanish-speaking students may find a discussion of the similarities and differences between English and Spanish cognates helpful.

English	Spanish
urbanization	urbanización
immigrant	inmigrante
emigration	emigración
commute	conmutar

BEFORE READING

Activate Prior Knowledge

Have students describe what comes to mind when they think of major cities and the areas that surround them. Encourage students to focus on people, types of buildings, transportation, sights, and sounds. Ask students how and why cities developed in the United States. Record their ideas on the board.

Introduce Target Vocabulary

Tell students they are about to read a selection about the growth of cities in the 1800s. Write the target vocabulary words on the board. Model the pronunciation of each word and have student volunteers repeat the word. Discuss the meaning of each word and, if necessary, write the definition next to the word.

Present Graphic Organizer

Provide each student with a copy of Vocabulary Graphic Organizer: Four Square, Teacher Guide page 78. Have students choose a target vocabulary word and write it in the center box. In each of the four squares of the chart, students should add information about the word to show they understand its meaning.

> Word and Definition Cards for Lesson 12 are on pages 121 and 122 of the Teacher Guide.

VOCABULARY STRATEGY: Word Roots

Write the target vocabulary words *immigrant* and *emigration* on the board. Ask students to identify the letter combinations these two words share (*migra*). Circle *migra* in each word. Explain that *migra* comes from the Latin word *migrare,* meaning "to change where one lives." The prefix *im-* indicates that an immigrant moves "in" to a place. The first part of emigrate is derived from the prefix *ex-*, which means "out," or "away from." Tell students that when they encounter unfamiliar words, they can try to figure out their meaning by looking for word roots that might be familiar to them.

The Growth of Cities

LESSON 12

urbanization	emigration	slum	ethnic group	suburb
immigrant	nativism	tenement	skyscraper	commute

What causes cities to grow? What happens when cities grow fast? Read this selection to learn why cities grew and changed in the late 1800s.

The Growth of Cities

As industry grew, factories needed more workers. Many Americans moved from farms to fill factory jobs. As a result, cities grew. The growth of cities is called **urbanization**. But factories needed even more workers.

Immigrants

Immigrants came to America to fill factory jobs. An **immigrant** is a person who comes to live in a country.

In the 1800s, millions of immigrants came to the East. They came from Germany and Ireland. Later, immigrants from Italy, Russia, and Poland arrived.

Immigrants also came to the West. They came from China, Japan, and Mexico.

Poverty was one reason for **emigration**, leaving one's country to live in another. Millions of Irish left Ireland to avoid starving when crops failed. Others left to find freedom. Over a million Jews left Russia to find religious freedom in the United States.

Immigrants were not always welcomed. Some people who had been born in the United States saw them as "outsiders." They believed that "native-born" people should be favored over immigrants. Many believers in **nativism** wanted to stop immigration.

Millions of immigrants came to the United States in the 1800s.

Life in the Cities

Cities could not change fast enough for all the people who were arriving. Housing was a big problem. As a result, slums developed. A **slum** is a poor, crowded part of a city. Many people in the slums lived in tenements. A **tenement** is a crowded apartment house.

In many cases, slums held people of the same ethnic group. An **ethnic group** is people with the same language, customs, culture, or country. For example, Russians chose to live with other Russians. Other groups did the same. They relied on one another for help.

In time, each new group of immigrants began to think of themselves as Americans. Eventually, ethnic groups got to know one another. They shared their customs and cultures.

Other Changes in Cities

Cities did not just get bigger. They also got taller. At the end of the 1800s, people began to build a new kind of building. It was called the **skyscraper**. Skyscrapers grew taller and taller. They changed the look of cities.

Transportation in cities also changed. Electric streetcars, or trolleys, allowed people to live farther from their jobs. A person could live in a suburb and still work in the city. A **suburb** is an area just beyond the city limits. The streetcar made the **commute**, the trip to and from work, possible.

Many immigrants lived in crowded tenements.

This early skyscraper was taller than everything around it.

 My Social Studies Vocabulary
Go to page 97 to list other words you have learned about the growth of cities.

DURING READING

Read the selection aloud to students, as they follow along in their books, pausing at the end of each paragraph or section. Review any words or concepts that students are having trouble understanding. Remind students that there is a glossary at the back of their book that contains all of the words that appear in boldfaced type in the lesson.

- Explain to students that *nativism* is a form of prejudice based on the idea that newcomers don't belong because they have different values or religions, or because they belong to a different ethnic group. In the United States, each wave of new immigrants faced nativism. Sometimes, nativism was expressed by an earlier group of immigrants!

- Tell students that the word *tenement* comes from the Latin *tenere,* meaning "to hold." The word *tenant,* which refers to a person who pays rent to live on or use a property, is also related to *tenere.* Have students connect the definitions of these words to the root word meaning.

- Remind students that a closed compound word is a word made by putting two smaller words together. Ask students which target vocabulary word is a closed compound (*skyscraper*). Ask them what words are used to create it (*sky* and *scraper*).

Have students read the selection again on their own.

AFTER READING

Review Graphic Organizer

Answer any questions students have about the reading selection. Then have students complete or review their graphic organizer and share it with the class.

Summarize

Have students work together to come up with either a written or an oral summary of the lesson. Encourage students to use the target vocabulary words as the basis of their summary. Have students share their summary with the class.

My Social Studies Vocabulary

Encourage students to turn to My Social Studies Vocabulary on page 97 of the student book and use the space provided to add other words related to the growth of cities.

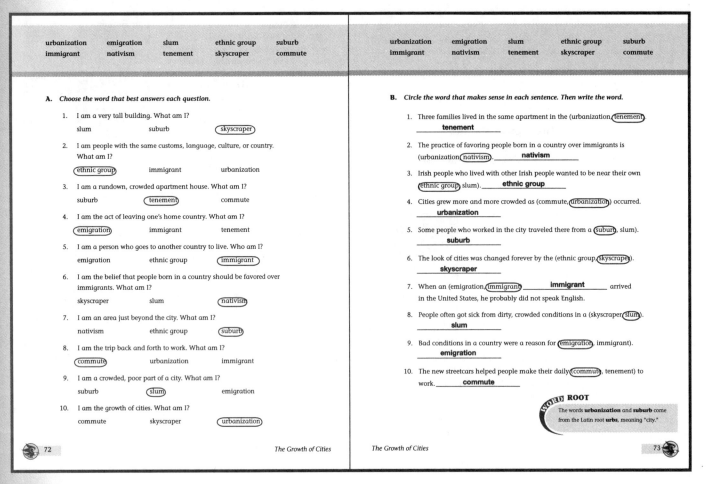

ACTIVITIES A–D

Encourage students to complete as many of the activities as possible. Remind students that they may refer to the Glossary at the back of their book as they complete the activities. Students may work independently, in small groups, or as a class. When students are done, discuss the answers for each activity.

Extensions

These extension ideas allow you to reuse or expand upon the activities. Share them with students who complete the activities before other students, or have students do them for additional practice with target vocabulary words.

A Take each target vocabulary word that is the answer to a question and ask an additional question about it. Exchange papers with a classmate and try to answer each other's questions.

B For each of the incorrect answers, write new sentences that would make sense. Leave blanks for the vocabulary words and see if a partner can choose the correct words.

C Look up five of the vocabulary words in a dictionary or encyclopedia. Find a new detail for each word such as an additional meaning or a different part of speech.

D Create a memory device that will help you to remember a word on the target vocabulary list that you find challenging.

WORD ROOT

Explain that *suburb* uses the Latin prefix *sub-*, which means "under." It is used when talking about something that is secondary to something else or that happens as a result of something else. Discuss how these meanings relate to the relationship between a city and a suburb. Ask students to come up with other words that use the prefix *sub-* (*subregion, substitute*).

C. *Choose the correct vocabulary word to complete each sentence.*

1. The neighbors spoke the same language and belonged to the same _____ethnic group_____ .

2. Just outside the city were the quiet streets of a _____suburb_____ .

3. People took an elevator to the top floor of the _____skyscraper_____ .

4. The family did not like their dirty rooms in the _____tenement_____ .

5. There were many overcrowded buildings in the _____slum_____ .

6. Mr. Laska made his _____commute_____ to the city by streetcar.

7. The family said that lack of food was a reason for _____emigration_____ from Ireland.

8. Hope for a better life was a reason for an _____immigrant_____ to come to the United States.

9. Immigrants were hurt by feelings of _____nativism_____ .

10. Changes in transportation and buildings were part of _____urbanization_____ .

Students' answers will vary.

D. *Use each pair of words in a sentence.*

1. skyscraper, urbanization
   The skyscraper was part of urbanization.

2. immigrant, nativism
   The immigrant needed a job, but nativism kept others from helping him.

3. commute, suburb
   Streetcars helped people make the commute from the suburb to the city.

4. emigration, ethnic group
   Even after emigration, some people lived among the same ethnic group they had lived with before leaving their country.

5. slum, tenement
   The tenement was located in the slum.

Write!
Write your response to the prompt on a separate sheet of paper. Use as many vocabulary words as you can in your writing.
Imagine that you were an immigrant to the United States during the late 1800s. Tell about why you left your country, how you traveled, and what you experienced in the United States.

Write!

Distribute Writing Graphic Organizer: Sequence Chart, Teacher Guide page 81. Tell students to use one box for each part of the journey from Europe to the United States—deciding to leave, traveling, seeing the city in the United States for the first time, and finding a new place to live.

Sample Answer

We were very poor, so my family chose emigration. We left Italy for the United States. The journey was long and hard. When we got to the United States, it was a different world. There were streetcars. We saw our first skyscraper. We saw nice homes in the suburbs. Our lives were hard, though. We lived in a dirty slum. Our home was a rundown tenement. We lived with our own ethnic group, other Italian people. We experienced nativism from people who spoke English.

TAKE-HOME ACTIVITY

Assign the Take-Home Activity to students for additional practice with the target vocabulary words. The reproducible Take-Home Activity for Lesson 12 is on page 95 of the Teacher Guide.

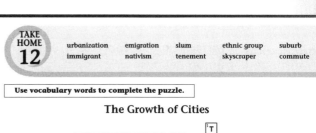

TAKE HOME 12

Use vocabulary words to complete the puzzle.

The Growth of Cities

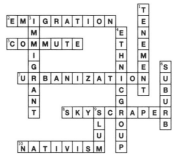

ACROSS

2 the leaving of one's country to live in another

5 the trip to and from one's home to a job

7 the growth of cities

8 a very tall building

10 the practice or policy of favoring native-born people over immigrants

DOWN

1 a crowded apartment building

3 a person who comes to live in a new country

4 people related by customs, language, culture, or country of origin

6 an area just beyond a city

9 a poor, crowded part of a city

Tell someone in your family what you have learned about the growth of cities.

95

LESSON 13

The Age of Reform

(Student Book pages 76–81)

Lesson Summary In the late 1800s, Southern states passed laws requiring literacy tests and poll taxes to prevent African Americans from voting. Jim Crow laws kept African Americans and whites separate in public places. Women also did not have equal rights. Many worked hard for suffrage. In large cities, reformers worked for change. Jane Addams founded a settlement house to provide services to poor people. Cities also suffered because of government corruption, kickbacks, and powerful political machines.

TARGET VOCABULARY

literacy test a test that checks a person's ability to read and write

poll tax money that must be paid to be able to vote

Jim Crow laws laws that separated African Americans and whites in public places

suffrage the right to vote

reformer a person who works for change

settlement house a place that offers services to help poor people

corruption lack of honesty

kickback payment to a person who controls a source of money

political machine an organized group of people in government with power

muckraker a writer who uncovers and writes about dishonest or unfair actions

COGNATES

Spanish-speaking students may find a discussion of the similarities and differences between English and Spanish cognates helpful.

English	Spanish
suffrage	sufragio
reformer	reformador
corruption	corrupción

BEFORE READING

Activate Prior Knowledge

Divide the class into small groups. Ask each group to brainstorm a response to the following question: If people are concerned about a community problem, what can they do to try to change things? Bring the class together and share ideas and examples.

Introduce Target Vocabulary

Tell students they are about to read a selection about a time of problems and reform in the United States. Write the target vocabulary words on the board. Model the pronunciation of each word and have student volunteers repeat the word. Discuss the meaning of each word and, if necessary, write the definition next to the word.

Present Graphic Organizer

Provide each student with a copy of Vocabulary Graphic Organizer: Vocabulary Circle, Teacher Guide page 79. Assign a target vocabulary word to each student, and have students write the word inside the center circle. As they read the lesson, students should add information about the word to the outer sections of the circle. They might write a definition, a sentence using the word, or draw a picture.

> Word and Definition Cards for Lesson 13 are on pages 123 and 124 of the Teacher Guide.

VOCABULARY STRATEGY: Roots, Prefixes, and Suffixes

Remind students that identifying the root of a word and knowing the meaning of any prefixes and suffixes added to the root can help them understand the meaning of an unknown word. For example, ask students to look at the target vocabulary word *reformer*. Explain to students that the root *form* means "to make or give shape to something." The prefix *re-* means "again." The suffix *-er* means, in this case, "one who performs an action." A *reformer,* therefore, is a person who works to make or give shape to something all over again. In other words, a reformer creates change.

literacy test   Jim Crow laws   reformer   corruption   political machine
poll tax   suffrage   settlement house   kickback   muckraker

*Some people didn't always have the right to vote in the United States.
Read this selection to learn about this problem and others
the United States faced in the late 1800s and early 1900s.*

The Age of Reform

Problems for African Americans

In the late 1800s, states in the South passed many unfair laws.
They tried to stop African Americans from voting. Some states said
voters had to pass a literacy test. A **literacy test** checks a person's
ability to read and write. Most slaves had not been taught to read
or write. Now they were free, but they could not pass a literacy test.

States also started a poll tax. A **poll tax** is money that must be
paid in order to vote. Many former slaves were too poor to pay the
tax. They could not vote.

Amendments to the Constitution
had given African Americans rights. But
later court rulings took away or limited
those rights. For example, in 1896, the
Supreme Court ruled that "separate
but equal" public places were legal. So,
some states passed **Jim Crow laws**.
These laws separated African Americans
and whites in public places. Trains had
separate cars for each race. The children
of each race went to separate schools.
There were even separate drinking
fountains for the two races.

*Jim Crow laws kept people
separate in public places.*

No Voting Rights for Women

Women also did not have equal rights. They could not
vote in national elections. The right to vote is called **suffrage**.
During the 1800s, women worked hard to be able to vote.
Over time, they reached their goal. In 1920, women were
able to vote in the national election.

*These women voted in a national
election for the first time in 1920.*

Jane Addams

The fast growth of cities brought many problems. Jane
Addams was a **reformer**, a person who works for change.
She helped to change the poor conditions she saw in her city,
Chicago. She founded Hull House. Hull House was a settlement
house. A **settlement house** offers services to help poor people.
Hull House offered classes. It had a playground and a music school.

Dishonest Government

Dishonest government also hurt cities. Many city officials
made money through corruption. **Corruption** is lack of honesty.
A corrupt city official might receive a kickback. A **kickback** is
a payment to a person who controls a source of money.

At this time, political machines ran many cities. A **political
machine** is an organized group of people in power. It trades
favors for votes. It makes unfair deals to stay in power.

Some writers wrote about political machines. They wrote
about other problems in the United States, too. A person
who wrote about dishonest or unfair dealings was called
a **muckraker**. The name comes from the dirty and often
impossible job of raking up mud.

*Upton Sinclair wrote about
unhealthy conditions in the
meat-packing industry.*

My Social Studies Vocabulary

Go to page 98 to list other words you have learned
about the age of reform.

DURING READING

Read the selection aloud to students, as they follow
along in their books, pausing at the end of each
paragraph or section. Review any words or concepts
that students are having trouble understanding.
Remind students that there is a glossary at the back
of their book that contains all of the words that
appear in boldfaced type in the lesson.

- Note that Jim Crow laws varied from state to state
  and even town to town. These laws were passed as
  late as the 1960s. Some laws also banned
  interracial marriage.

- Point out to students that some states gave women
  suffrage before a national amendment was passed.
  California, for example, gave women the right to
  vote in state elections in 1911.

- Point out that two target vocabulary words are
  compound words that are descriptive. Have
  students identify them (*kickback, muckraker*). Ask
  students to demonstrate the images that come to
  mind when they read these words. How do the
  images help them to understand the meanings of
  the words? (*A person with a rake scrapes up and*

*gathers muck, or mud and filth, just as a writer might
gather information about corruption. Kickback suggests
someone moving forward while kicking something
backwards—just as a person getting ahead due to
special favors pays back the one who offered the favors.*)

Have students read the selection again on their own.

AFTER READING

Review Graphic Organizer

Answer any questions students have about the reading
selection. Then have students complete or review their
graphic organizer and share it with the class.

Summarize

Have students work together to come up with either
a written or an oral summary of the lesson. Encourage
students to use the target vocabulary words as the
basis of their summary. Have students share their
summary with the class.

My Social Studies Vocabulary

Encourage students to turn to My Social Studies
Vocabulary on page 98 of the student book and use
the space provided to add other words about the age
of reform.

The Age of Reform

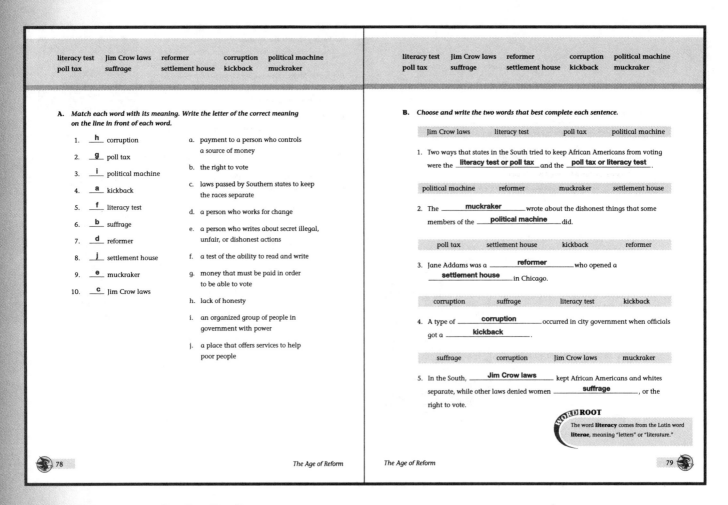

The worksheet pages shown (pages 78 and 79):

literacy test   Jim Crow laws   reformer   corruption   political machine
poll tax   suffrage   settlement house   kickback   muckraker

A. Match each word with its meaning. Write the letter of the correct meaning on the line in front of each word.

1. __h__ corruption
2. __g__ poll tax
3. __i__ political machine
4. __a__ kickback
5. __f__ literacy test
6. __b__ suffrage
7. __d__ reformer
8. __j__ settlement house
9. __e__ muckraker
10. __c__ Jim Crow laws

a. payment to a person who controls a source of money
b. the right to vote
c. laws passed by Southern states to keep the races separate
d. a person who works for change
e. a person who writes about secret illegal, unfair, or dishonest actions
f. a test of the ability to read and write
g. money that must be paid in order to be able to vote
h. lack of honesty
i. an organized group of people in government with power
j. a place that offers services to help poor people

B. Choose and write the two words that best complete each sentence.

| Jim Crow laws | literacy test | poll tax | political machine |

1. Two ways that states in the South tried to keep African Americans from voting were the __literacy test or poll tax__ and the __poll tax or literacy test__.

| political machine | reformer | muckraker | settlement house |

2. The __muckraker__ wrote about the dishonest things that some members of the __political machine__ did.

| poll tax | settlement house | kickback | reformer |

3. Jane Addams was a __reformer__ who opened a __settlement house__ in Chicago.

| corruption | suffrage | literacy test | kickback |

4. A type of __corruption__ occurred in city government when officials got a __kickback__.

| suffrage | corruption | Jim Crow laws | muckraker |

5. In the South, __Jim Crow laws__ kept African Americans and whites separate, while other laws denied women __suffrage__, or the right to vote.

WORD ROOT
The word **literacy** comes from the Latin word **literae**, meaning "letters" or "literature."

The Age of Reform   78   79   The Age of Reform

ACTIVITIES A–D

Encourage students to complete as many of the activities as possible. Remind students that they may refer to the Glossary at the back of their book as they complete the activities. Students may work independently, in small groups, or as a class. When students are done, discuss the answers for each activity.

Extensions

These extension ideas allow you to reuse or expand upon the activities. Share them with students who complete the activities before other students, or have students do them for additional practice with target vocabulary words.

A Turn each definition into a complete sentence by adding a subject (the target vocabulary word) and a verb.

B Choose one vocabulary word you would like to look up on the Internet. List the questions you have about it.

WORD ROOT

Ask students to explain how the Latin root *literae* connects to the meaning of *literacy* in *literacy test*. Then ask them to use the prefix *il-*, meaning *not*, to form an antonym of *literacy*. Have students look in the dictionary to find additional words using the root *literae*, such as *literal* and *literary*.

C Organize the words into groups according to meaning or subject matter. The words within each group should all be related in some way.

D Use one of the target vocabulary words to create a poem about the lesson or some part of it. Write the word vertically down a sheet of paper, one letter per line. Have each letter serve as the first letter of a line of the poem.

C. *Choose the correct vocabulary word to complete each sentence.*

1. The city official received money as a __kickback__ .

2. The poor people received help at the __settlement house__ .

3. A story about dishonesty in government was written by a __muckraker__ .

4. During the 1800s, African Americans and women did not have __suffrage__ .

5. Solving problems is the work of a __reformer__ .

6. City governments were weakened by wrongdoing and other __corruption__ .

7. In the South, African Americans attended separate schools because of __Jim Crow laws__ .

8. Many former slaves who could not read or write failed the __literacy test__ for voting.

9. Some people could not afford to pay the __poll tax__ , so they could not vote.

10. Buying votes was one way that a __political machine__ stayed in power.

80   The Age of Reform

Students' answers will vary.

D. *Use each word in a sentence that shows you understand the meaning of the word.*

1. poll tax __Mr. Jeffers couldn't pay the poll tax, so he couldn't vote.__

2. reformer __The reformer wanted to help poor people find better housing.__

3. political machine __Members of the political machine made deals to stay in power.__

4. Jim Crow laws __Jim Crow laws said that people of different races could not sit in the same car of a train.__

5. settlement house __The settlement house helped the poor people in many different ways.__

6. muckraker __The muckraker told about how the city leader cheated to get money.__

7. literacy test __If you can't read, you can't pass a literacy test.__

8. corruption __No one trusted the city leaders because of stories of corruption.__

9. kickback __The city official got a kickback from the deal.__

10. suffrage __Women worked toward the goal of suffrage.__

Write!

Write your response to the prompt on a separate sheet of paper. Use as many vocabulary words as you can in your writing.

You are a muckraker in the year 1900. Describe a topic you would like to write an article about.

The Age of Reform   81

Write!

Distribute Writing Graphic Organizer: Topic Web, Teacher Guide page 80. In the top circle, students should briefly describe the topic they wish to write about. In the lower circles, they should give details they would include in writing about the topic.

Sample Answer

   As a muckraker, I would like to write about city leaders who get rich on money that should go to the city. I would like to write about each kickback they take. They stay in power because the political machine is so strong. We need a city reformer to change this soon! There is too much corruption in our city government.

TAKE-HOME ACTIVITY

Assign the Take-Home Activity to students for additional practice with the target vocabulary words. The reproducible Take-Home Activity for Lesson 13 is on page 96 of the Teacher Guide.

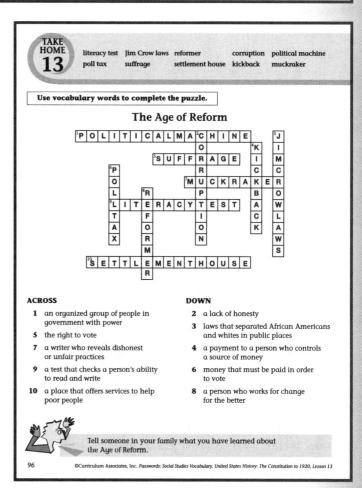

TAKE HOME 13

Use vocabulary words to complete the puzzle.

The Age of Reform

ACROSS

1 an organized group of people in government with power

5 the right to vote

7 a writer who reveals dishonest or unfair practices

9 a test that checks a person's ability to read and write

10 a place that offers services to help poor people

DOWN

2 a lack of honesty

3 laws that separated African Americans and whites in public places

4 a payment to a person who controls a source of money

6 money that must be paid in order to vote

8 a person who works for change for the better

Tell someone in your family what you have learned about the Age of Reform.

96   ©Curriculum Associates, Inc. Passwords: Social Studies Vocabulary, United States History: The Constitution to 1920, Lesson 13

The Age of Reform

LESSON 14

Becoming a World Power

(Student Book pages 82–87)

Lesson Summary The United States grew larger and stronger through imperialism. In 1898, the United States annexed Hawaii. The United States then joined Cuba and the Philippines in a war against Spain. As a result, the United States gained Puerto Rico and the Philippines. Cuba became a United States protectorate. The United States also battled Colombia and later built the Panama Canal. Some people favored isolationism; they did not want to form alliances with other nations.

TARGET VOCABULARY

imperialism the practice of one country taking over a weaker country

revolt a violent action by people against their ruler

invest to put money in a business deal to make a profit

guerrilla someone who carries out surprise attacks

cavalry soldiers on horseback

protectorate a country that is protected and controlled by a stronger country

negotiate to talk about a matter to reach an agreement

isolationism a belief in staying out of the business or politics of other nations

foreign outside of a country

alliance a group of countries with a common purpose

COGNATES

Spanish-speaking students may find a discussion of the similarities and differences between English and Spanish cognates helpful.

English	Spanish
imperialism	imperialismo
guerrilla	guerrilla
cavalry	caballería
protectorate	protectorado
isolationism	aislacionismo
alliance	alianza

BEFORE READING

Activate Prior Knowledge

Ask students to write down words and images that come to mind when they think of the words *world power*. What do these words mean to students? What do they believe are good and bad uses of power in different situations? Encourage them to explain their responses. Write their ideas on the board and return to them when the class completes the lesson.

Introduce Target Vocabulary

Tell students they are about to read a selection about the United States becoming a world power. Write the target vocabulary words on the board. Model the pronunciation of each word and have student volunteers repeat the word. Discuss the meaning of each word and, if necessary, write the definition next to the word.

Present Graphic Organizer

Distribute copies of Vocabulary Graphic Organizer: Vocabulary Map, Teacher Guide page 77. Have students choose a target vocabulary word and write the word in the center box. As students work through the lesson, they should add as much information as they can about their target vocabulary word to each area of the chart.

> Word and Definition Cards
> for Lesson 14 are on pages 125 and 126
> of the Teacher Guide.

VOCABULARY STRATEGY: Print Features

Review with students why a word might appear in boldfaced type in a textbook. (*It is an important new word. The word will be defined within the text.*) Tell students that they can often find the meaning of a boldfaced word close to where the word appears in the text. Have students locate five boldfaced words that are defined within the text. Ask them to draw an arrow from each word to the part of the sentence that gives the meaning of the word.

Becoming a World Power

LESSON 14

imperialism	invest	cavalry	negotiate	foreign
revolt	guerrilla	protectorate	isolationism	alliance

How does a young nation become powerful? How does it grow larger? Read this selection to learn how the United States became a world power.

Becoming a World Power

The United States grew until it reached the Pacific Ocean. Then people began to think about new ways of growing. They were in favor of imperialism. **Imperialism** is the practice of one country taking over a smaller or weaker country. For example, in 1898, the United States took over Hawaii.

How does this picture illustrate American imperialism?

The Spanish-American War

The United States also got land by going to war. At the end of the 1800s, Spain ruled Cuba. The Cuban people wanted to be free. They started a revolt against Spain. A **revolt** is a violent action by people against their ruler. Many Americans wanted to help the Cubans with their revolt. But Americans who had invested money in Cuban businesses wanted the United States to help Spain. To **invest** is to put money in a business deal to make a profit.

When an American ship sank in Cuba, the United States blamed Spain. In 1898, it declared war on Spain.

Spain also controlled the Philippine Islands, in Asia. The United States fought in the war there as well as in Cuba. Guerrillas from the Philippines helped the Americans. A **guerrilla** is a person who carries out surprise attacks.

The biggest battle of the Spanish-American War took place in Cuba. On July 1, 1898, the **cavalry**, soldiers on horseback, captured San Juan Hill. Spain could not hold on to Cuba.

The soldiers that captured San Juan Hill were known as the "Rough Riders."

The war was soon over. In 1899, the United States gained Puerto Rico and the Philippines. Cuba became a United States protectorate. A **protectorate** is a country that is protected and controlled by a stronger country.

The Panama Canal

The United States wanted to build a canal across Panama. At the time, Colombia ruled Panama. President Roosevelt tried to **negotiate** with Colombia to buy some land. But the country's leader did not want to talk about the matter to reach an agreement. Then Panama revolted against Colombia. Panama and the United States fought against Colombia and won. The new nation of Panama then let the United States build the canal.

The Panama Canal

Voices of Protest

Some people did not like the way that the United States had gained power. They favored **isolationism**. They wanted to stay out of the politics and business of other countries. They did not want to fight in **foreign** wars, wars outside the country. They also did not want to join the alliances forming in Europe. An **alliance** is a group of countries with a common purpose. Alliances helped lead to World War I.

My Social Studies Vocabulary

Go to page 96 to list other words you have learned about how the United States became a world power.

DURING READING

Read the selection aloud to students, as they follow along in their books, pausing at the end of each paragraph or section. Review any words or concepts that students are having trouble understanding. Remind students that there is a glossary at the back of their book that contains all of the words that appear in boldfaced type in the lesson.

- Ask students to identify the target vocabulary words ending with the suffix *-ism. (imperialism, isolationism)* Explain that *-ism* is a suffix meaning "action or process" or "condition or quality."
- Tell students that *guerrilla* comes from *guerra,* the Spanish word meaning "war." It means "little war." Explain to students that the word is often used in the phrase *guerilla warfare* to describe a particular style of fighting that includes small bands of soldiers conducting surprise raids and attacks in order to wear down the enemy.
- Show students a map of the world or a globe and help them find the places mentioned in the reading selection: *Hawaii, Cuba, the Philippines, Panama.*

Have students read the selection again on their own.

AFTER READING

Review Graphic Organizer

Answer any questions students have about the reading selection. Then have students complete or review their graphic organizer and share it with the class.

Summarize

Have students work together to come up with either a written or an oral summary of the lesson. Encourage students to use the target vocabulary words as the basis of their summary. Have students share their summary with the class.

My Social Studies Vocabulary

Encourage students to turn to My Social Studies Vocabulary on page 98 of the student book and use the space provided to add other words about the United States becoming a world power.

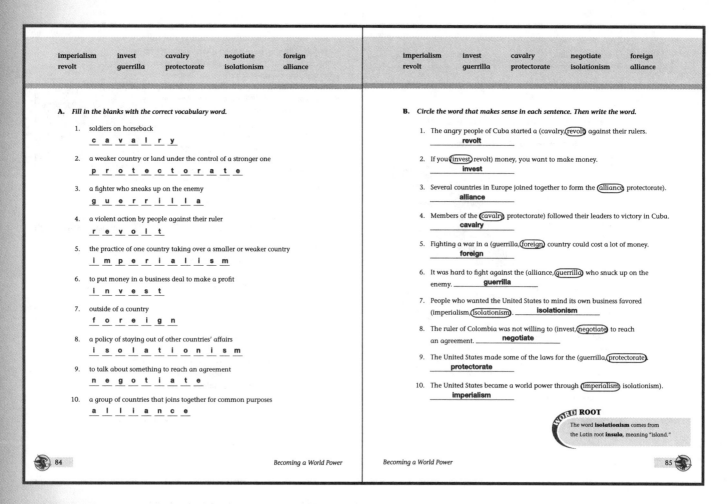

A. *Fill in the blanks with the correct vocabulary word.*

1. soldiers on horseback

   c a v a l r y

2. a weaker country or land under the control of a stronger one

   p r o t e c t o r a t e

3. a fighter who sneaks up on the enemy

   g u e r r i l l a

4. a violent action by people against their ruler

   r e v o l t

5. the practice of one country taking over a smaller or weaker country

   i m p e r i a l i s m

6. to put money in a business deal to make a profit

   i n v e s t

7. outside of a country

   f o r e i g n

8. a policy of staying out of other countries' affairs

   i s o l a t i o n i s m

9. to talk about something to reach an agreement

   n e g o t i a t e

10. a group of countries that joins together for common purposes

    a l l i a n c e

B. *Circle the word that makes sense in each sentence. Then write the word.*

1. The angry people of Cuba started a (cavalry, revolt) against their rulers.
   revolt

2. If you (invest, revolt) money, you want to make money.
   invest

3. Several countries in Europe joined together to form the (alliance, protectorate).
   alliance

4. Members of the (cavalry, protectorate) followed their leaders to victory in Cuba.
   cavalry

5. Fighting a war in a (guerrilla, foreign) country could cost a lot of money.
   foreign

6. It was hard to fight against the (alliance, guerrilla) who snuck up on the enemy. **guerrilla**

7. People who wanted the United States to mind its own business favored (imperialism, isolationism). **isolationism**

8. The ruler of Colombia was not willing to (invest, negotiate) to reach an agreement. **negotiate**

9. The United States made some of the laws for the (guerrilla, protectorate). **protectorate**

10. The United States became a world power through (imperialism, isolationism). **imperialism**

WORD ROOT

The word **isolationism** comes from the Latin root **insula**, meaning "island."

ACTIVITIES A–D

Encourage students to complete as many of the activities as possible. Remind students that they may refer to the Glossary at the back of their book as they complete the activities. Students may work independently, in small groups, or as a class. When students are done, discuss the answers for each activity.

Extensions

These extension ideas allow you to reuse or expand upon the activities. Share them with students who complete the activities before other students, or have students do them for additional practice with target vocabulary words.

A Put the target words in alphabetical order.

B Find smaller words within the target vocabulary words, such as *protect, protector, rate, ate,* and *tar* in *protectorate.*

WORD ROOT

Have students explain how the meaning of *isolationism* relates to the meaning of its Latin root. *(An island is not connected to other land. Believers in isolationism do not want their country to form connections with other countries.)*

C Scramble the letters of each target vocabulary word. List the scrambled words in random order on a sheet of paper. Exchange scrambled word lists with a partner and try to unscramble each other's words.

D Choose one sentence and add two more sentences that provide more information about the topic or the target vocabulary word.

imperialism	invest	cavalry	negotiate	foreign
revolt	guerrilla	protectorate	isolationism	alliance

C. *Choose the correct vocabulary word to complete each sentence.*

1. The United States became more powerful through _____**imperialism**_____.

2. People who wanted the United States to stay out of world affairs believed in _____**isolationism**_____.

3. The nations had many of the same interests so they formed an _____**alliance**_____.

4. The Battle of San Juan Hill was fought by soldiers in the _____**cavalry**_____.

5. People who believed in isolationism did not want Americans to be involved in _____**foreign**_____ wars.

6. The United States looked after its _____**protectorate**_____.

7. The troops were surprised by the attack of the _____**guerrilla**_____.

8. If a country's ruler refuses to talk, you cannot _____**negotiate**_____ with him.

9. Cubans who disliked their Spanish rulers joined in the _____**revolt**_____.

10. A person who had decided to _____**invest**_____ in Cuba wanted the United States to side with Spain.

---

imperialism	invest	cavalry	negotiate	foreign
revolt	guerrilla	protectorate	isolationism	alliance

Students' answers will vary.

D. *Use each word in a sentence that shows you know the meaning of the word.*

1. foreign ___**The United States has fought many wars in foreign lands.**___

2. negotiate ___**The leader of Colombia did not want to negotiate a sale.**___

3. protectorate ___**The protectorate had to obey the country that controlled it.**___

4. isolationism ___**Keeping out of other countries' problems far from home is isolationism.**___

5. invest ___**People often invest in companies in other countries.**___

6. alliance ___**The alliance consisted of six countries.**___

7. imperialism ___**Strong countries may use imperialism to get stronger.**___

8. cavalry ___**The cavalry rode to the battle on the hill.**___

9. guerrilla ___**The guerrilla attacked when no one expected danger.**___

10. revolt ___**The Cuban people carried out a revolt against Spain.**___

 Write!

Write your response to the prompt on a separate sheet of paper. Use as many vocabulary words as you can in your writing.

Imagine that you live in 1907. How do you feel about the United States becoming a world power? State your opinion and explain it.

Write!

Distribute Writing Graphic Organizer: Two-Column Chart, Teacher Guide page 83. Tell students to write "Becoming a World Power" at the top of the chart. On one side of the chart, have them list what they see as the positive aspects of becoming a world power. On the other side of the chart, they should write what they see as the negative aspects.

Sample Answer

I am glad the United States is a world power because we have more money and jobs at home. Still, I don't think we have the right to annex other lands. If other people revolt against their rulers, we should stay neutral. It is not our business. Why should we send our army, navy, and cavalry to fight in faraway places? This is imperialism.

On the other hand, I don't believe in isolationism. We should do business in other countries. That will make our country richer.

TAKE-HOME ACTIVITY

Assign the Take-Home Activity to students for additional practice with the target vocabulary words. The reproducible Take-Home Activity for Lesson 14 is on page 97 of the Teacher Guide.

TAKE HOME 14

imperialism	invest	cavalry	negotiate	foreign
revolt	guerrilla	protectorate	isolationism	alliance

Use vocabulary words to complete the puzzle.

Becoming a World Power

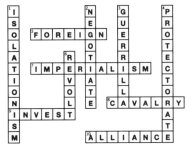

ACROSS

5. outside one's own country
7. the practice of one country taking over a smaller or weaker country
8. soldiers on horseback
9. to put money into a business deal to make a profit
10. a group of nations that join together for a common purpose

DOWN

1. the belief in staying out of the business and politics of other countries
2. to discuss a matter to reach an agreement
3. a person who carries out surprise attacks
4. a country that is protected and controlled by a stronger country
6. a violent action of people against their ruler

 Tell someone in your family what you have learned about the United States becoming a world power.

©Curriculum Associates, Inc. *Passwords: Social Studies Vocabulary, United States History: The Constitution to 1920, Lesson 14*   97

Becoming a World Power

LESSON 15

World War I

(Student Book pages 88–93)

Lesson Summary World War I started in Europe in 1914. The use of tanks, airplanes, and trench warfare made fighting difficult. A stalemate caused the war to drag on. Americans hoped diplomacy would keep them out of the war, but in 1917 the United States entered the war. Propaganda helped raise support for the war and for mobilization. The war ended in 1918. Casualties on both sides were high. Germany, one of the losing nations, was ordered to pay reparations.

TARGET VOCABULARY

combat armed fighting

diplomacy the making of peaceful agreements among nations

trench warfare fighting from long, narrow ditches, or trenches, dug in the ground

front the place where the fighting is going on in a war

stalemate a state of no progress or change

propaganda anything used to influence people's thinking or actions

slogan a short saying that is easy to remember

mobilization the raising, training, and supplying of an army

casualties people who are killed and wounded

reparations payments for damages by a defeated nation in war

COGNATES

Spanish-speaking students may find a discussion of the similarities and differences between English and Spanish cognates helpful.

English	Spanish
combat	combate
trench warfare	guerra de trincheras
propaganda	propaganda
slogan	eslogan

BEFORE READING

Activate Prior Knowledge

Ask students to describe ways in which a government might spark an interest among its people to join or support a war effort. List their ideas on the board. Return to students' lists as they complete the lesson, adding details and examples to their previous responses.

Introduce Target Vocabulary

Tell students they are about to read a selection about World War I. Write the target vocabulary words on the board. Model the pronunciation of each word and have student volunteers repeat the word. Discuss the meaning of each word and, if necessary, write the definition next to the word.

Present Graphic Organizer

Provide each student with a copy of Vocabulary Graphic Organizer: Vocabulary Circle, Teacher Guide page 79. Assign each student a target vocabulary word. Have students write their target vocabulary word inside the center. As they read the lesson, students should add as much additional information as they can about the word in the outer sections.

> Word and Definition Cards
> for Lesson 15 are on pages 127 and 128
> of the Teacher Guide.

VOCABULARY STRATEGY: Use Pictures

Explain to students that photographs, illustrations, and other types of pictures, especially in textbooks, can provide readers with a visual explanation for unfamiliar words. Point out that in this lesson, the image of soldiers fighting from a trench and the propaganda posters featuring slogans support and clarify definitions given in the text. Remind students to refer to pictures, here and in their other reading, to get a better idea of the meaning of unfamiliar words.

| combat | trench warfare | stalemate | slogan | casualties |
| diplomacy | front | propaganda | mobilization | reparations |

In the summer of 1914, World War I began in Europe. Why would the United States want to stay out of the war at first? Why would it eventually decide to join in? Read this selection to learn why the United States finally entered World War I.

World War I

By 1907, Europe was split into two sides. Austria-Hungary, Germany, and Italy were on one side. Great Britain, France, and Russia were on the other side. Each side built up weapons and large armies. Each side was ready for **combat**, or armed fighting. Americans did not want to take sides. They hoped that diplomacy would win out. **Diplomacy** is the making of peaceful agreements between nations.

However, in 1914, a member of the royal family of Austria-Hungary was shot. World War I began.

New Ways of Fighting

World War I was a bloody and awful war. One reason was new war machines, such as tanks and airplanes. Another reason was trench warfare. In **trench warfare**, soldiers fire guns at one another from ditches, or trenches, dug in the ground.

Soldiers dug trenches in the ground.

In World War I, soldiers on the front mainly stayed in the trenches. A **front** is the place where the fighting is going on.

Trench warfare made it hard for either side to win the war. The front often stayed in the same place for months at a time. This was a **stalemate**, a state of no progress or change. The two sides were dug into the ground, and neither side could move. The war dragged on.

The United States Enters the War

Many Americans wanted to stay out of the war. Then Germany sank a British ship with many American passengers. Some Americans began to change their minds.

The United States government used propaganda to change more people's minds. **Propaganda** is anything used to influence people's thinking or actions. Propaganda often uses signs and slogans. A **slogan** is a short saying. It is easy to remember.

The United States entered the war in 1917. The government faced the huge job of mobilization. **Mobilization** is the raising, training, and supplying of an army. Thousands of American soldiers were sent to Europe. The United States, Great Britain, France, and other nations won the war.

The War Ends

The war ended in 1918. The costs of the war were very high. There were about 42 million casualties. **Casualties** are the dead and wounded. World War I was such a huge war, it was called "the war to end all wars."

Germany was one of the nations that lost the war. After the war, Germany was not allowed to have an army. It also had to pay reparations to Great Britain, France, and other nations. **Reparations** are payments for damages made by a defeated nation in war. Reparations left Germany poor and bitter. In 1939, Germany would be at war in Europe again.

These World War I posters were pro-war propaganda.

My Social Studies Vocabulary
Go to page 98 to list other words you have learned about World War I.

DURING READING

Read the selection aloud to students, as they follow along in their books, pausing at the end of each paragraph or section. Review any words or concepts that students are having trouble understanding. Remind students that there is a glossary at the back of their book that contains all of the words that appear in boldfaced type in the lesson.

- Note that *front* commonly means "the forward part" of something, such as the front of a building. In a military sense, a front is the forward part of the army. Behind the action at the front, there are soldiers resting or being treated for injuries, food and weapons supply chains, and so on.

- Tell students that the word *propaganda* is related to the word *propagate,* which means "to spread" and "to make widely known." Ask them to explain how this meaning relates to the purpose and function of propaganda. Have students discuss why the posters shown on page 89 are examples of propaganda. Then have them identify and discuss examples of propaganda in today's world.

- Tell students that the word *reparations* comes from the Latin word *reparare,* meaning "to repair." Have students explain how the meaning of *reparations* connects to the meaning of *repair.*

Have students read the selection again on their own.

AFTER READING

Review Graphic Organizer

Answer any questions students have about the reading selection. Then have students complete or review their graphic organizer and share it with the class.

Summarize

Have students work together to come up with either a written or an oral summary of the lesson. Encourage students to use the target vocabulary words as the basis of their summary. Have students share their summary with the class.

My Social Studies Vocabulary

Encourage students to turn to My Social Studies Vocabulary on page 98 of the student book and use the space provided to add other words about World War I.

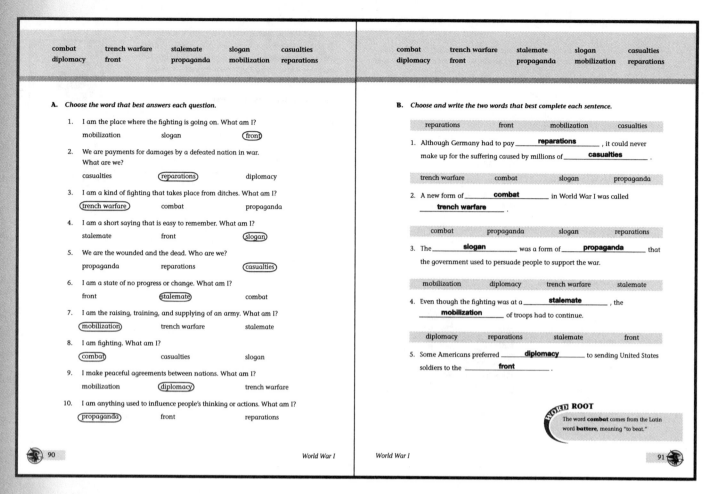

| combat | trench warfare | stalemate | slogan | casualties |
| diplomacy | front | propaganda | mobilization | reparations |

A. *Choose the word that best answers each question.*

1. I am the place where the fighting is going on. What am I?
   mobilization   slogan   (front)

2. We are payments for damages by a defeated nation in war. What are we?
   casualties   (reparations)   diplomacy

3. I am a kind of fighting that takes place from ditches. What am I?
   (trench warfare)   combat   propaganda

4. I am a short saying that is easy to remember. What am I?
   stalemate   front   (slogan)

5. We are the wounded and the dead. Who are we?
   propaganda   reparations   (casualties)

6. I am a state of no progress or change. What am I?
   front   (stalemate)   combat

7. I am the raising, training, and supplying of an army. What am I?
   (mobilization)   trench warfare   stalemate

8. I am fighting. What am I?
   (combat)   casualties   slogan

9. I make peaceful agreements between nations. What am I?
   mobilization   (diplomacy)   trench warfare

10. I am anything used to influence people's thinking or actions. What am I?
    (propaganda)   front   reparations

90   World War I

B. *Choose and write the two words that best complete each sentence.*

| reparations | front | mobilization | casualties |

1. Although Germany had to pay **reparations**, it could never make up for the suffering caused by millions of **casualties**.

| trench warfare | combat | slogan | propaganda |

2. A new form of **combat** in World War I was called **trench warfare**.

| combat | propaganda | slogan | reparations |

3. The **slogan** was a form of **propaganda** that the government used to persuade people to support the war.

| mobilization | diplomacy | trench warfare | stalemate |

4. Even though the fighting was at a **stalemate**, the **mobilization** of troops had to continue.

| diplomacy | reparations | stalemate | front |

5. Some Americans preferred **diplomacy** to sending United States soldiers to the **front**.

WORD ROOT
The word **combat** comes from the Latin word **battere**, meaning "to beat."

World War I   91

ACTIVITIES A–D

Encourage students to complete as many of the activities as possible. Remind students that they may refer to the Glossary at the back of their book as they complete the activities. Students may work independently, in small groups, or as a class. When students are done, discuss the answers for each activity.

Extensions

These extension ideas allow you to reuse or expand upon the activities. Share them with students who complete the activities before other students, or have students do them for additional practice with target vocabulary words.

A Put the target vocabulary words in alphabetical order.

B For each item, create a new sentence that uses the other two words. Leave blanks where the target words should go, then exchange papers with a partner and complete each other's paper sentences.

C Create a word-search puzzle with the target vocabulary words. Exchange puzzles with a classmate and see who can find all the words first.

D Rewrite each of your sentences as a question that has either a "yes" or "no" answer.

WORD ROOT

Point out to students that **combat** may be used as a noun, as it is in this lesson, or as a verb. As a verb, *combat* means "to fight against." Combat may also be used as an adjective, as in "combat boots," "combat pay," or "combat team." Ask students to think of other words that come from the root *battere* (*battle, batter*).

combat	trench warfare	stalemate	slogan	casualties
diplomacy	front	propaganda	mobilization	reparations

C. *Choose the correct vocabulary word to complete each sentence.*

1. "Be all you can be" is an example of a _____**slogan**_____.

2. The natural disaster resulted in a large number of _____**casualties**_____.

3. Great Britain received _____**reparations**_____ from Germany after World War I.

4. The United States hoped that _____**diplomacy**_____ would avoid a war.

5. After the United States declared war, the _____**mobilization**_____ of troops increased.

6. Soldiers who took part in _____**trench warfare**_____ fought from ditches.

7. The armies were trained and ready for _____**combat**_____.

8. Both sides wanted to end the _____**stalemate**_____ and to start making progress.

9. Soldiers often lose their lives at the _____**front**_____.

10. Some people were convinced to fight by posters and other _____**propaganda**_____.

World War I

---

combat	trench warfare	stalemate	slogan	casualties
diplomacy	front	propaganda	mobilization	reparations

Students' answers will vary.

D. *Use each word in a sentence that shows you know the meaning of the word.*

1. stalemate **Neither side made progress during the stalemate.**

2. combat **Many of the soldiers were eager for combat.**

3. casualties **The battle was over quickly, and there were few casualties.**

4. slogan **"Give blood, save a life" is a slogan.**

5. diplomacy **Diplomacy can save lives, but war takes lives.**

6. trench warfare **The fighting stayed in the same place for a long time because of trench warfare.**

7. propaganda **Governments use propaganda to persuade people to support some wars.**

8. reparations **Germany had to pay reparations for the damages it had caused.**

9. mobilization **The mobilization of troops is a complicated task.**

10. front **The soldier went to the front to fight in the battle.**

Write!

Write your response to the prompt on a separate sheet of paper. Use as many vocabulary words as you can in your writing.

Imagine that you are a soldier fighting in the trenches in World War I. Tell some of your thoughts and feelings about the war.

World War I

Write!

Distribute Writing Graphic Organizer: Main Idea and Details Chart, Teacher Guide page 82. In each Main Idea box, students should write an opinion or feeling about some aspect of the war. In the corresponding Details boxes, they should write details that support their main ideas.

Sample Answer

I am in a trench at the front. Trench warfare makes it very difficult to make any progress. We are at a stalemate now and have been at a stalemate for a long time. I would prefer combat to waiting in the trenches.

I am sorry I listened to the propaganda about why we had to fight the war. There are so many casualties. I hope the war ends soon.

TAKE-HOME ACTIVITY

Assign the Take-Home Activity to students for additional practice with the target vocabulary words. The reproducible Take-Home Activity for Lesson 15 is on page 98 of the Teacher Guide.

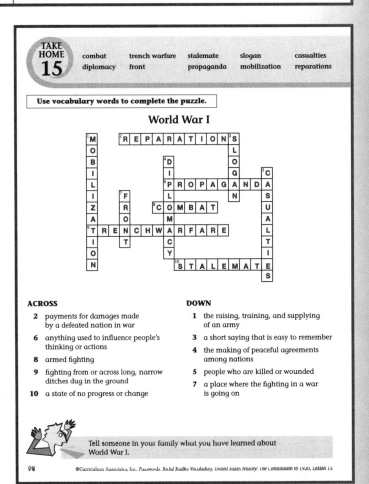

TAKE HOME 15

combat	trench warfare	stalemate	slogan	casualties
diplomacy	front	propaganda	mobilization	reparations

Use vocabulary words to complete the puzzle.

World War I

ACROSS

2 payments for damages made by a defeated nation in war

6 anything used to influence people's thinking or actions

8 armed fighting

9 fighting from or across long, narrow ditches dug in the ground

10 a state of no progress or change

DOWN

1 the raising, training, and supplying of an army

3 a short saying that is easy to remember

4 the making of peaceful agreements among nations

5 people who are killed or wounded

7 a place where the fighting in a war is going on

Tell someone in your family what you have learned about World War I.

©Curriculum Associates, Inc. Passwords: Social Studies Vocabulary, United States History: The Constitution to 1920, Lesson 15

World War I

Vocabulary Graphic Organizer: Word Chart

Word	
Definition	
Examples	
Sentence	

Draw a Picture

Name _____ Date _____

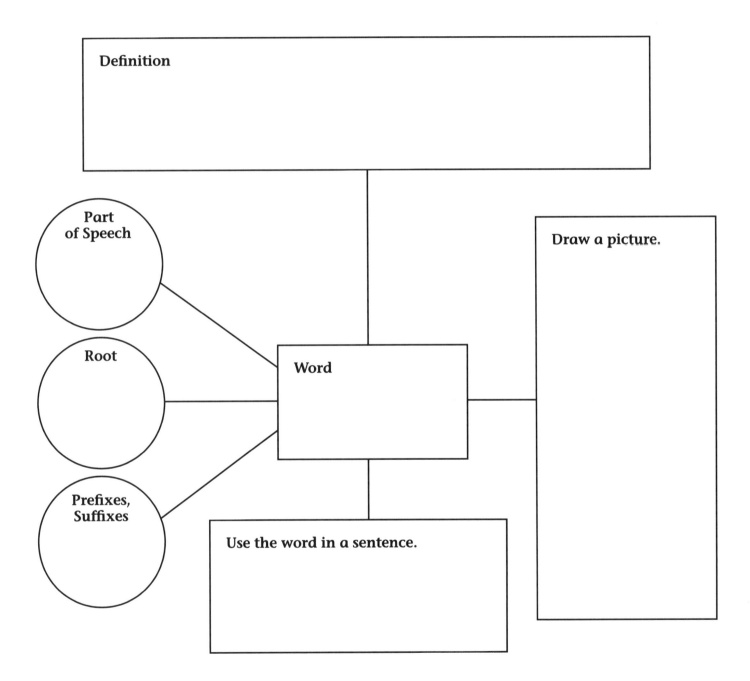

Definition

Part of Speech

Root

Prefixes, Suffixes

Word

Draw a picture.

Use the word in a sentence.

Name _____ Date _____

Draw a picture.	Use the word in a sentence.

Word

Definition	Examples

©Curriculum Associates, Inc. *Passwords: Social Studies Vocabulary, United States History: The Constitution to 1920*

Name _____ Date _____

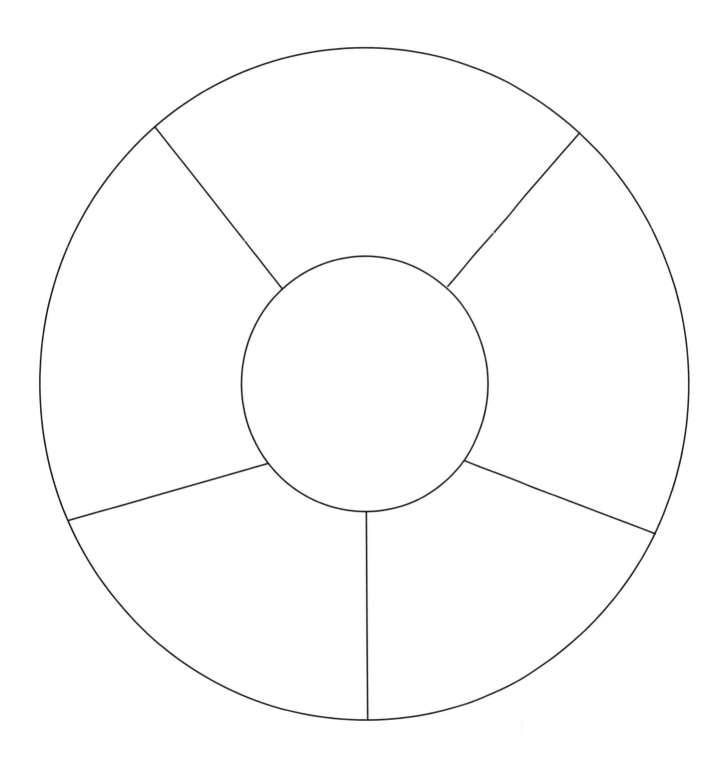

Writing Graphic Organizer: Topic Web

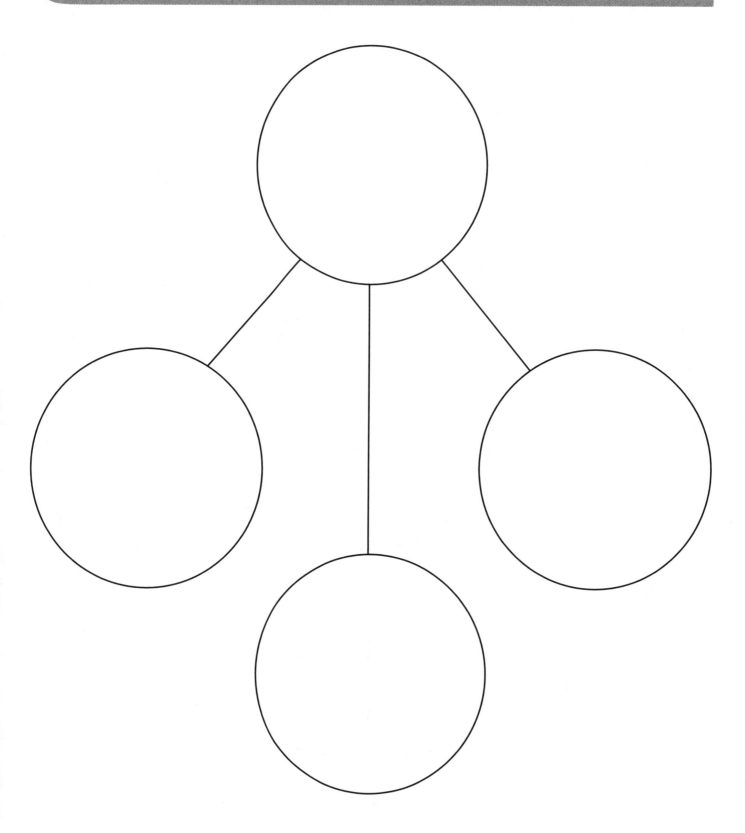

Name _____ Date _____

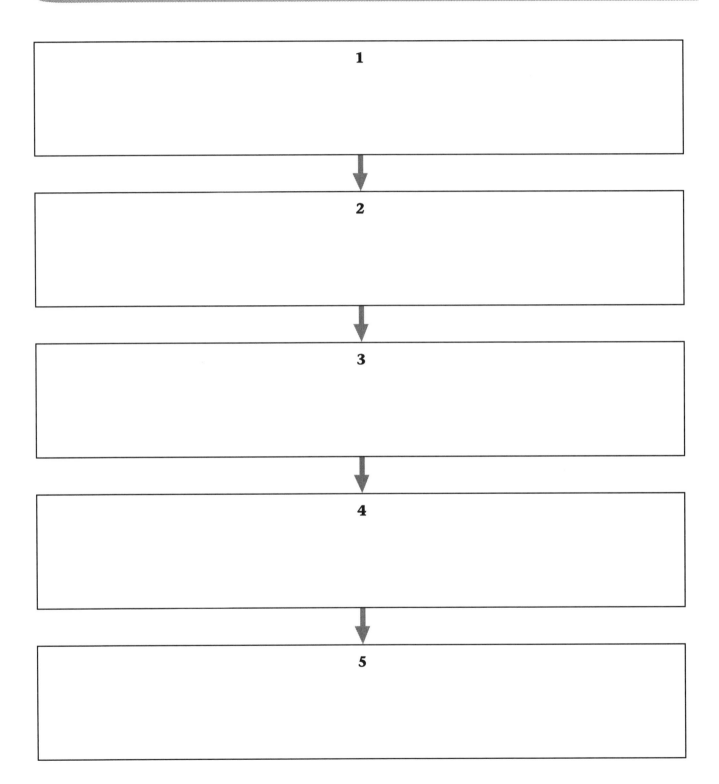

1

↓

2

↓

3

↓

4

↓

5

Name _____ Date _____

Writing Graphic Organizer: Main Idea and Details Chart

Main Idea	Details
1. _____ _____ _____ _____ _____ _____	_____ _____ _____ _____ _____
2. _____ _____ _____ _____ _____ _____ _____	_____ _____ _____ _____ _____ _____
3. _____ _____ _____ _____ _____ _____	_____ _____ _____ _____ _____

Name _____ Date _____

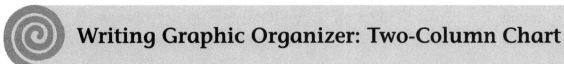

Writing Graphic Organizer: Two-Column Chart

colony   Great Awakening   political   revolution   rights
preach   authority   independence   declaration   clause

Use vocabulary words to complete the puzzle.

The Break from Great Britain

ACROSS

3 freedom from control

7 a section of a document

8 an area ruled by another country

9 official power

10 a period of renewed interest in religion

DOWN

1 freedoms that are protected by law

2 a serious statement about something

4 to talk about religious subjects

5 a war against one's own government

6 having to do with the government

Tell someone in your family what you have learned about the break from Great Britain.

constitution   Magna Carta   document   taxation   pilgrim

foundation   parliament   subject   monarchy   compact

Use vocabulary words to complete the puzzle.

The Roots of the Constitution

ACROSS

3 rule by one person

5 a person who travels a long distance for religious reasons

8 a set of laws and ideas that describe a government

9 a group of people chosen to make laws

10 under the power of another

DOWN

1 an agreement

2 a list of political rights created by English nobles and signed by the king in 1215

4 the base upon which something is built

6 a formal piece of writing

7 the art of raising money to support the government

Tell someone in your family what you have learned about the roots of the Constitution.

confederation   compromise   reserved powers   checks and balances
convention   democracy   separation of powers   amendment
delegates   federalism

Use vocabulary words to complete the puzzle.

The Constitution

ACROSS

2 a system in which each branch of government can limit the actions of the other branches

5 a change to a document

8 a system of government in which power is shared between states and national government

9 a group of independent states working together

10 the separation of the government into three branches

DOWN

1 powers given to the states

3 a meeting that has a particular purpose

4 an agreement in which each side gets part of what it wants

6 people chosen to speak and vote for a group

7 a form of government that gets its power from the people

Tell someone in your family what you have learned about the Constitution.

executive branch administration controversy tariff neutrality
cabinet treasury revenue excise tax policy

Use vocabulary words to complete the puzzle.

The Early Years of the United States

ACROSS

2 a president's time in office

3 a tax on goods brought into a country

6 the part of the government that carries out laws

8 public disagreement between two sides with opposite views

9 a policy of not taking sides during a war

DOWN

1 the group of people who give advice to the president and make up the heads of departments

3 the department in charge of collecting taxes and managing public funds

4 money paid to the government by a maker or seller of a product

5 income that a government collects to pay for public expenses

7 a plan of action

Tell someone in your family what you have learned about the early years of the United States.

blockade   embargo   territory   doctrine   spoils system
impress   armistice nationalism landslide   veto

Use vocabulary words to complete the puzzle.

The New Nation and the World

ACROSS

1 a statement of government policy

7 to prevent ships from entering or leaving a port

8 to vote "no"

9 an agreement to stop fighting

10 the practice of giving government jobs to supporters

DOWN

2 land under control of a country

3 pride in one's country

4 to force a person into military service

5 a ban on goods leaving a country

6 the winning of an election by a very large majority of votes

Tell someone in your family what you have learned about the new nation and the world.

| opportunity | adjoining | turnpike | canal | ordinance |
| pioneer | frontier | technology | freight | homeland |

Use vocabulary words to complete the puzzle.

Settling the West

ACROSS

2 a waterway that connects two bodies of water

4 an area of few people at the edge of a settled area

7 the land that a person comes from

9 a chance to make money or to better oneself

10 the use of scientific knowledge to make machines and tools

DOWN

1 a rule or law

3 next to

5 a road that travelers have to pay to use

6 one of the first people to settle an area

8 goods carried by a ship, truck, train, or airplane

Tell someone in your family what you have learned about settling the West.

boundary   expansion   land grant   mass production   capitalism

Manifest Destiny   latitude   annex   economy   entrepreneur

Use vocabulary words to complete the puzzle.

An Expanding Nation

ACROSS

2 a system in which privately owned businesses control production

5 the belief that the United States had the right to extend its boundaries from the Atlantic Ocean to the Pacific Ocean

8 a border

9 someone who starts a business, taking all the risks but getting all the profit

10 all the business dealings of a country or state

DOWN

1 public land given by a government

3 to add to something larger or more important

4 the process of making things in large amounts, usually by machine

6 an increase in size

7 the distance north or south of the equator

Tell someone in your family what you have learned about the expanding nation.

boom	abolitionist	fugitive		conductor	radical
abolish	sectionalism	Underground Railroad		sue	secede

Use vocabulary words to complete the puzzle.

The Road to War

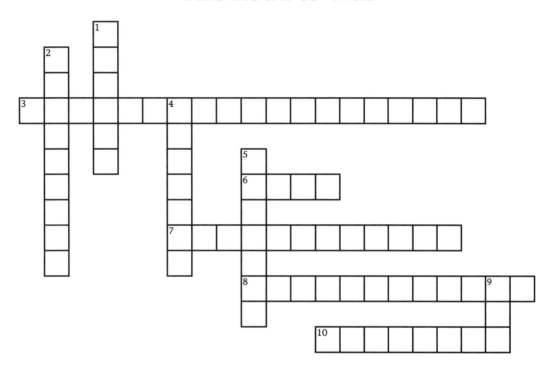

ACROSS

3 a system of people who helped slaves to escape from the South

6 a sudden increase

7 a person who worked to end slavery

8 loyalty to one's own region rather than the country as a whole

10 a person who runs away

DOWN

1 to withdraw from a country to form a new country

2 a person who led a group of slaves to freedom on the Underground Railroad

4 a person who is in favor of extreme changes

5 to put an end to something

9 to bring legal action to settle a disagreement

Tell someone in your family what you have learned about the road to war.

civil war	Union	emancipation	riot	total war
Confederacy	defensive	draft	turning point	surrender

Use vocabulary words to complete the puzzle.

The Civil War

ACROSS

4 a major change

6 a war between groups in the same country

7 the group of Southern states that left the nation

9 the act of setting people free

10 a crowd of people who become out of control

DOWN

1 done to protect against attack

2 the practice of attacking the enemy's civilians and resources as well as the army

3 to declare that an enemy has won and that fighting can stop

5 the nation, or the Northern states, after the South left the nation

8 to choose someone from a group to serve in the armed forces

Tell someone in your family what you have learned about the Civil War.

assassination   freedmen   tenant farmer   inherit   carpetbagger
Reconstruction   sharecropper   black codes   segregation   scalawag

---

Use vocabulary words to complete the puzzle.

Reconstruction

ACROSS

4 to get something from someone after her or she has died

7 a Northerner who went to the South during Reconstruction

8 the killing of a public figure

9 the plan to rebuild the South and bring it back into the Union

10 a farmer who works someone else's land in return for a share of the crop

DOWN

1 the practice of separating people by race

2 a Southern white person who was in favor of Reconstruction

3 a farmer who pays rent to work someone else's land

5 former slaves

6 laws that limited the rights of freedmen

Tell someone in your family what you have learned about Reconstruction.

industrialization   transcontinental   regulate   sweatshop   strike
invention   corporation   monopoly   labor union   panic

Use vocabulary words to complete the puzzle.

Industrialization

ACROSS

2 a company that controls an industry by getting rid of its competition

4 a time when businesses fail, jobs disappear, and banks close

8 a stopping of work to force company owners to make changes for the better

9 the change from farming to industry

10 going across the continent

DOWN

1 an original idea for making new things

3 a group of workers who join together to bring changes

5 a business owned by many people

6 to control

7 a small factory or mill with poor working conditions

Tell someone in your family what you have learned about industrialization.

urbanization   emigration   slum   ethnic group   suburb
immigrant   nativism   tenement   skyscraper   commute

Use vocabulary words to complete the puzzle.

The Growth of Cities

ACROSS

2 the leaving of one's country to live in another

5 the trip to and from one's home to a job

7 the growth of cities

8 a very tall building

10 the practice or policy of favoring native-born people over immigrants

DOWN

1 a crowded apartment building

3 a person who comes to live in a new country

4 people related by customs, language, culture, or country of origin

6 an area just beyond a city

9 a poor, crowded part of a city

Tell someone in your family what you have learned about the growth of cities.

literacy test   Jim Crow laws   reformer   corruption   political machine

poll tax   suffrage   settlement house kickback   muckraker

Use vocabulary words to complete the puzzle.

The Age of Reform

ACROSS

1 an organized group of people in government with power

5 the right to vote

7 a writer who reveals dishonest or unfair practices

9 a test that checks a person's ability to read and write

10 a place that offers services to help poor people

DOWN

2 a lack of honesty

3 laws that separated African Americans and whites in public places

4 a payment to a person who controls a source of money

6 money that must be paid in order to vote

8 a person who works for change for the better

Tell someone in your family what you have learned about the Age of Reform.

imperialism   invest   cavalry   negotiate   foreign
revolt   guerrilla   protectorate   isolationism   alliance

Use vocabulary words to complete the puzzle.

Becoming a World Power

ACROSS

5 outside one's own country

7 the practice of one country taking over a smaller or weaker country

8 soldiers on horseback

9 to put money into a business deal to make a profit

10 a group of nations that join together for a common purpose

DOWN

1 the belief in staying out of the business and politics of other countries

2 to discuss a matter to reach an agreement

3 a person who carries out surprise attacks

4 a country that is protected and controlled by a stronger country

6 a violent action of people against their ruler

Tell someone in your family what you have learned about the United States becoming a world power.

combat trench warfare stalemate slogan casualties
diplomacy front propaganda mobilization reparations

Use vocabulary words to complete the puzzle.

World War I

ACROSS

2 payments for damages made by a defeated nation in war

6 anything used to influence people's thinking or actions

8 armed fighting

9 fighting from or across long, narrow ditches dug in the ground

10 a state of no progress or change

DOWN

1 the raising, training, and supplying of an army

3 a short saying that is easy to remember

4 the making of peaceful agreements among nations

5 people who are killed or wounded

7 a place where the fighting in a war is going on

Tell someone in your family what you have learned about World War I.

colony

independence

preach

revolution

Great
Awakening

declaration

authority

rights

political

clause

freedom from control

an area ruled by another country

a war against one's own government

to talk about religious subjects

a serious statement about something

a period of renewed interest in religion in the early 1700s

freedoms that are protected by law

official power

a section of a document

having to do with the government

constitution	subject
foundation	taxation
Magna Carta	monarchy
parliament	pilgrim
document	compact

under the power of another	a set of laws and ideas that describe a government
the act of raising money to support the government	the base upon which something is built
rule by one person, such as a king or queen	a list of political rights created by English nobles and signed by the king in 1215
a person who travels a long distance for religious reasons	a group of people chosen to make laws
an agreement	a formal piece of writing

confederation

democracy

convention

reserved
powers

compromise

separation
of powers

delegates

checks and
balances

federalism

amendment

a system of government run by the people who live under it

a group of independent states that work together

powers given to the states

a meeting for a particular purpose

the separation of the government into three branches

an agreement in which each side gives up something

a system in which each branch of government can limit the actions of the other branches

people chosen to speak and vote for a group

a change to a document

a system of government in which power and duties are shared between states and national governments

executive branch

revenue

cabinet

tariff

administration

excise tax

treasury

neutrality

controversy

policy

the income that a government collects to pay for public expenses

the part of the government that carries out laws

a tax on goods brought into a country

a group of people who give advice to the president and make up the heads of departments

money paid by a maker or seller of a product

the time during which a United States president holds office

a policy of not taking sides in a war

the department in charge of collecting taxes and managing public funds

a plan of action

a public disagreement between two sides with opposite views

©Curriculum Associates, Inc. *Passwords: Social Studies Vocabulary, United States History: The Constitution to 1920, Lesson 4—Word Cards*

blockade

nationalism

impress

doctrine

embargo

landslide

armistice

spoils system

territory

veto

pride in one's country

to prevent ships from entering or leaving a port

a statement of government policy

to force a person into military service

the winning of an election by a very large majority of votes

a ban on exporting goods

the practice of giving jobs to supporters

an agreement to stop fighting

to say or vote "no"

land under the control of a country

©Curriculum Associates, Inc. *Passwords: Social Studies Vocabulary, United States History: The Constitution to 1920, Lesson 5—Word Cards*

opportunity

technology

pioneer

canal

adjoining

freight

frontier

ordinance

turnpike

homeland

the use of scientific knowledge to make machines and tools

a chance to make money or to better oneself

a waterway dug across land that connects two bodies of water

one of the first people to settle an area

goods carried by ship, truck, train, or airplane

next to

a law or rule passed by a government

an area with few people at the edge of a settled region

the land that a person comes from

a road that travelers have to pay to use

©Curriculum Associates, Inc. *Passwords: Social Studies Vocabulary, United States History: The Constitution to 1920, Lesson 6—Word Cards*

boundary	annex
Manifest Destiny	mass production
expansion	economy
latitude	capitalism
land grant	entrepreneur

to add to something larger or more important

a border

the process of making large quantities of things by machine

the belief that the United States had the right to extend its boundaries from the Atlantic Ocean to the Pacific Ocean

all the business dealings of a country or state

the act of increasing in size

a system in which privately owned businesses control the production of goods

the distance north or south of the equator

someone who starts a business, taking all of the risks but getting all of the profits

public land given to individuals by a government

boom

Underground Railroad

abolish

conductor

abolitionist

sue

sectionalism

radical

fugitive

secede

a system of people who helped slaves escape

a sudden increase in production

a person who led slaves to freedom on the Underground Railroad

to put an end to something

to bring legal action to settle a disagreement

a person who worked to end slavery

a person who is in favor of extreme changes

loyalty to one's region rather than the whole country

to leave one country and form a new one

a person who runs away

civil war	draft
Confederacy	riot
Union	turning point
defensive	total war
emancipation	surrender

to choose someone from a group to serve in the armed forces

a war between groups in the same country

a crowd of people who become out of control

the group of Southern states that left the United States

an event that changes the way things are going

the Northern states that remained in the United States during the Civil War

a war against an enemy's civilians and resources as well as its army

done to protect against attack

to declare that one's enemy has won and that fighting can stop

the act of setting people free

assassination

black codes

Reconstruction

segregation

freedmen

inherit

sharecropper

carpetbagger

tenant farmer

scalawag

laws that limited the rights of freedmen

the killing of a public figure

the practice of separating people by race

the plan to rebuild the South and bring it back into the United States

to get something from someone after he or she has died

former slaves

a Southern name for a Northerner who moved to the South during Reconstruction

a farmer who works someone else's land in return for a share of the crops

a Southern name for a Southern white person who was in favor of Reconstruction

a farmer who pays rent to work someone else's land

industrialization	monopoly
invention	sweatshop
transcontinental	labor union
corporation	strike
regulate	panic

| a company that completely controls an industry or business | the change from farming to industry |

| a small factory or mill with poor working conditions | an original idea for a new process or product |

| a group of workers who join together to bring changes | going across the continent |

| a stopping of work by workers to get better working conditions or higher pay | a business owned by many people, each of whom own a share of the business |

| a time when businesses fail, jobs disappear, and banks close | to control through laws |

urbanization	tenement
immigrant	ethnic group
emigration	skyscraper
nativism	suburb
slum	commute

a crowded apartment building

the growth of cities

people with the same customs, language, culture, or country

a person who comes to a new country to live

a very tall building

the leaving of one's own country to live in another country

an area just beyond a city

the practice or policy of favoring native-born people over immigrants

the trip to and from one's home to a job

a poor, crowded part of a city

literacy test	settlement house
poll tax	corruption
Jim Crow laws	kickback
suffrage	political machine
reformer	muckraker

a place set up to provide services to poor people in cities

a test of the ability to read and write

lack of honesty

a tax paid in order to vote

a payment to a person who controls a source of money

the laws passed by states to keep African Americans and whites separate

an organized group of people in government with power

the right to vote

a writer who reveals dishonest or unfair practices

a person who works for change

imperialism	protectorate
revolt	negotiate
invest	isolationism
guerrilla	foreign
cavalry	alliance

a country that is protected and controlled by a stronger one

the practice of one country taking over smaller or weaker countries

to talk about a matter to reach an agreement

a violent action of people against their ruler

a belief in staying out of the business or politics of other nations

to put money into a business deal to make a profit

outside of a country

a soldier who makes surprise attacks

a group of nations that join together for a common purpose

soldiers who fight on horseback

 Passwords: Social Studies Vocabulary, United States History: The Constitution to 1920, Lesson 14—Word Cards

combat

propaganda

diplomacy

slogan

trench
warfare

mobilization

front

casualties

stalemate

reparations

anything used to influence
people's thoughts or actions

armed fighting

a short saying that is easy to
remember

the making of peaceful agreements
among nations

the raising, training, and supplying
of an army

fighting from or across long,
narrow ditches dug in the ground

the people who are injured or killed

the place where the fighting in a
war is going on

payments for damages by a defeated
nation in a war

a state of no progress or gain